W9-ANV-549

Xmas 1986

A Doctor's Calling

Other books by Morris Gibson
One Man's Medicine
Doctor in the West

A Doctor's Calling

Morris Gibson

Douglas & McIntyre
Vancouver/Toronto

Copyright © 1986 by William Morrison Gibson
86 87 88 89 90 5 4 3 2 1

Douglas & McIntyre Ltd., 1615 Venables Street,
Vancouver, British Columbia   V5L 2H1

Canadian Cataloguing in Publication Data

Gibson, Morris.
    A doctor's calling

    ISBN 0-88894-521-3
    1. Gibson, Morris. 2. Physicians – Great
    Britain – Biography. 3. Physicians – Alberta –
    Biography. I. Title.
    R464.G48A33 1986   610'.92'4   C86-091399-6

Published simultaneously in the United States of America by Beaufort Books Publishers, New York.

Cover design and illustration by Paul Bacon
Typeset by Pièce de Résistance
Printed and bound in the United States of America.

In the text, names and descriptions of characters have been fictionalized except for those physicians and public figures whose identities it would be impossible to conceal.

TO FRIENDSHIP.
"There's nothing worth the wear of winning
but laughter and the love of friends."
Hilaire Belloc

Acknowledgements

I wish to express my gratitude to James Herriot for his warm encouragement; to Cy Goodwin who has once again so generously and patiently typed and prepared my manuscript; to Derek Cassels, Editor, the *Medical Post*, for permission to use some previously published material; to Janet for her patience and inspiration, and to many friends who have allowed me to write about them.

A Doctor's Calling

Chapter One

The Devil lived in our church. I knew that for a fact, because every Sunday the Reverend Arthur Alexander (M.A., B.D., Edinburgh) said so.

To be precise, Satan lived underneath the church. The entrance to Hell was on the floor, just in front of the pulpit, behind the heavy old oak communion table.

By the end of his Sunday morning sermons our minister had worked himself into a terrible state. His face, normally so placid and kindly, became suffused with emotion and exertion as he harangued his congregation, thumping so heavily on the great pulpit Bible that its satin bookmarks, one scarlet and the other purple, danced in the still church air.

Then, at the climax of the sermon he would lean over the pulpit, point to that spot on the floor and roar, "There, my friends, is the way to Hell, and the sinners amongst you will surely go there!"

At this point, overcome by emotion and grief for the delinquencies of his flock, he would throw himself back on to the pulpit bench and bury his head in his hands.

Mostly the congregation seemed to face its fate with stolid indifference, but there were times when, stricken by the vehemence of their minister's eloquence, people would sit for minutes in dumbfounded silence.

It was one Saturday morning that I was filled by the knowledge of my impending doom. Tomorrow I would go to Hell! The Devil, belching fire and flaming cinders, would leap from his hole, reach up to the balcony and drag me down to everlasting purgatory.

For that week I had sinned. I was a gangster and a thief. Aged ten. *I had stolen the coal money!*

I was the leader of my gang. On the Tuesday of that fateful week I had led my outfit against that of Jimmy Seath who lived across the road.

Our battles were as ritualistic and usually as harmless as those of Fijian high school teachers demonstrating ancient war dances; but little boys, if worked up enough, are not above kicking other little boys' shins, or even blacking eyes, and my men had ignominiously fled the field, pursued by screeching little savages.

I had not stayed, heroically and alone, to face the enemy. I was fleeter of foot than most.

There was to be a return battle on Friday. Jimmy Seath's lot were to play the part of the English. It was therefore imperative that we, the Scots, should be victorious.

Perhaps it was a mistaken sense of patriotism that led me to sin. The situation was desperate, and unless reinforcements were found, defeat and disgrace awaited me. That was when I stole the coal money.

It was a custom in our house that father would regularly place two shillings and sixpence under the marble clock that graced our mantelpiece. Mother retrieved the coins on Thursdays and paid Mr. Lang, our coalman.

Although accusations of forgetfulness and carelessness were made and parried by my parents, the mystery of the missing coins was never solved; and on Friday after school, I quietly retrieved my wooden sword from its hiding place in the depths of the raspberry patch and led my men into action.

The perfidious English, faced by a veritable army of Scots and deserters from their own ranks, turned and ran, pursued by my valiant countrymen, each of whom clutched in his good right hand a penny bar of nut milk chocolate. The coal money had been reallocated for military purposes.

But the joys of conquest, in greater events than this skirmish, are short-lived.

On Saturday I began to feel unwell. I developed abdominal pain. It became worse and on Sunday morning I was unable to leave my bed. My loving and concerned parents conferred over me, then decided they should send for the doctor — something that was never done lightly, especially on the Sabbath! The family's attendance at church was cancelled.

In due course, gruff, kindly old Dr. Duff arrived. After his preliminary ceremonials had been completed, my parents watched in silence as he examined me. Then they all retired to the balcony outside my bedroom.

"Well, Gibson," said the doctor to my father, mother having retired to make a cup of tea for our visitor, "it's not an appendix."

"I'm glad to hear that, but what is it?"

There followed my first indication that even great men can be fallible.

"It's green apples," said Dr. Duff with certainty. "I told you, Gibson, when you planted these trees, that you were putting in the wrong apples. These are cooking apples. You can't blame the boy if he gorged himself on them. Give him fluids today and keep him in bed. He'll be all right by tomorrow."

I was the object of solicitous attention all that day.

But I knew I didn't suffer from acute appendicitis or green apples. What I suffered from was acute fear of the Devil!

On Monday morning I had recovered enough to return to school, but it was an uneasy week and on Saturday my ailment recurred.

This time, however, there was to be no reprieve. On Sunday morning I was taken to church. I had confided in no one. It was a lonely dread for a little boy and I dragged myself into church and up the cold stone stairway to our pew, which occupied part of the front row of the balcony. I had an almost unrestricted view of the Devil's entrance to this mortal world.

The service got under way, my terror increasing with the singing of every hymn. Just before the Reverend Alexander launched into his sermon, Mother passed along the Sunday candies. This was a weekly operation that called for skill and stealth. We must not be seen to be chewing and above all we must not be heard, for Mr. Alexander in his pulpit possessed the eyes of an eagle and the ears of a cougar. The merest distraction would be noted and frowned upon.

Therefore the candies were always Scotch Imperial Mints, which could be sucked. Even the paper bag containing them was carefully chosen, being of such age and softness that it made the merest rustle as it passed from hand to hand. But I did not want a candy that day and saw my mother's amazement and concern at my refusal.

The sermon reached the climax.

"Hell," cried the minister, "will claim its due."

Terror-struck, I clutched the ledge that held the hymn books.

"Even he," I told myself, "is going to have a job to pry me loose."

"For the Devil," declaimed the minister, "walketh about, seeking whom he may devour!"

But the Devil didn't turn up, even at the third time of asking, so to speak, and at the end of the service, light-headed with relief, I almost stumbled down the stairs and into the grey, drizzling Scottish Sabbath, thrust my fists into my pockets and decided for all time that if the Devil existed at all, he wasn't always on the job.

It was my first, and far from my last, experience of what today we call psychosomatic illness.

I had beaten the Devil. All the same, like so many Scots, I never quite escaped from the fear of his displeasure.

Chapter Two

I was sixteen before I spoke to Dr. Duff again, though I sometimes saw him when he called at our home to discuss with my father some matter of mutual interest. On those occasions I made myself scarce, for Dr. Duff was not one of those modern young physicians who wear casual slacks and coloured sports shirts and keep toys in their offices for the diversion of children. He was tall, stern, impeccably dressed in dark suits, and he seldom smiled.

And yet I had the greatest faith in him. He had delivered me, and when as a child I developed pneumonia, my parents told me how he sat with me for hours waiting for "the crisis" in the infection. When I was a boy — and a young medical student — that crisis was all-important. It signified the point at which the patient's temperature must either recede or increase, marking the beginning of resolution of the disease, or deterioration towards coma and death.

Scientifically Dr. Duff had done little for me. What few drugs there were then were almost useless. A failing heart might be stimulated through the crisis, but in the 1920s that was about all there was for the patient.

When I was studying medicine, our knowledge of disease was elementary by today's standards. The antibiotics and sulpha drugs were years away. A good constitution and an active immune system were often all that stood between the patient and death.

But spiritually our family doctor, I am still convinced, did a great deal for me. The fear of devoted parents communicated itself to me as a child and I remember how anxiously, even in convalescence, I awaited the arrival of the doctor.

And that stern, silent man was kind. He encouraged me, told me to keep my spirits up, and assured me that all would be well.

A few years ago I was browsing through the Tate Gallery in London, when I came across Sir Luke Fildes's famous painting, "The Doctor."

It shows a dimly lit bedroom with a desperately ill child lying propped up in bed. In the shadows stand the anxious parents, and by the bedside sits the doctor, chin in hand, his intent gaze fixed upon the child. I have heard this work described by some as a great example of English portraiture, by others as "a piece of Victorian corn."

I am no art critic, but as I looked at that painting I suddenly recalled my own childhood pneumonia and how I had so anxiously awaited the daily arrival of the one man who was my guardian against death, and who gave me hope.

Sir Luke saw in that doctor an artist in his own right and put into perpetuity the image of a dedicated physician, one of a profession that has enjoyed high public esteem.

Men like Sir Luke's subject and like Dr. Duff, practised the "art and science of medicine." Despite their often woefully inadequate knowledge of disease, the best of them, if maintaining a distance from their patients, and an authoritarianism that masked their own uncertainties, were understanding and compassionate human beings. There was a mystique to the practice of medicine, masking an ignorance of science.

Medicine is still not so much a science that we physicians can afford to neglect the art.

But philosophy was far from the mind of the sixteen-year-old boy who long ago knocked at the door of Dr. Duff's house, that low, grey stone building where the surrounding trees shut out what sun there was.

My father had told me that the doctor wanted to have a talk with me that evening, and I was puzzled. Why should Dr. Duff want to see me?

His housekeeper, severely dressed in black as became her position, ushered me along the dark corridor to the doctor's study, where he sat at his roll-top desk, its top strewn with books and papers.

He had been a handsome man. His clean-shaven face, firm mouth and deep-set eyes could inspire either fear or confidence, but in those six years that had elapsed since he diagnosed my case of "green apples" he had grown frail, old and bent with arthritis.

Courteously he bade me sit and said, "I won't be long — I'm just finishing a letter."

Not knowing what was to come, I waited uneasily, my discomfiture increasing when momentarily he stopped writing and silently inspected me.

Suddenly he put down his pen, turned towards me and said, "So, young man, I suppose you're wondering what all this is about?" Without waiting for an answer he went on. "Your father and I have been having a talk and we've come to the conclusion it's time you thought of your future. Have you given any thought to that?''

I had to admit I hadn't. Life seemed very secure, and at sixteen the future could take care of itself.

But the doctor had other ideas. "I think you should consider becoming a doctor," he said abruptly, and suddenly he launched into a dissertation on the rewards of being a physician, turning from that to the future of medicine. How prophetic he was! As a doctor, and long after his time, he told me, I would see deadly diseases conquered and surgical wonders performed.

Years later my father told me how failing health had forced the doctor to retire and how he had died, a poor, lonely and largely forgotten man far from the town to which he had devoted his life.

But what a picture he painted for me that night! And yet medicine had hardly entered the twentieth century. Surgery had made great strides, but anaesthesia was still a terrifying ordeal for patients who were "put to sleep," choking, fighting for breath, often held down on the operating table by students or nurses as ether or chloroform was crudely poured onto a face mask. The hazards of anaesthesia were considerable, even for the healthy, and second or third experiences were dreaded.

The "wonder" drugs were years away, and sophisticated methods of investigation were in their infancy. Physicians relied largely on their powers of observation, on those tests that were available, and on clinical acumen often acquired by grim and heartbreaking experience. Death was taken for granted by both doctors and patients in a way that would never be accepted today.

But Dr. Duff kindled a flame in me that night, and I walked home with my mind racing. In due course I applied for entry to Glasgow University's School of Medicine, and was accepted, why or how I will never know.

Medical students today, certainly in North America, seem to possess formidable academic backgrounds, mostly in the sciences. I still have difficulty with simple arithmetic. Somehow, however, having attained the requisite academic requirements for university entrance, I found myself in 1934, at the age of eighteen, a first-year medical student.

We, youngsters then, suffered none of the ordeals that face today's applicants for "places." Today the intellectual requirements are very high, and while a degree in science is often an asset, I'm not sure it's altogether a good idea. We can be too scientific, too technological in our approach to the practice of medicine.

After a lifetime as a physician, I am more convinced than ever of the value of well-trained family doctors who treat their patients and families as a whole, people who can be relied upon to practise competent medicine and seek the right kind of specialist care when necessary. Such physicians might even be the better for not having a specialized scientific background!

After all, there is a story that one distinguished English medical school, which was also noted for its rugby football team, chose its students from the ranks of good football players—and that school graduated many distinguished medical men!

Today's applicants are required to appear before medical school admissions committees, usually composed of faculty members and laymen. They are sometimes appraised by psychologists and are often required to submit theses outlining their reasons for wanting to become doctors. Obviously a desire to help suffering mankind must be cited as a shining urge. Some overdo this.

In later life in Canada I became a university teacher, then head of a department and a member of the executive council of the faculty. I had heard rumours. With age comes skepticism, and one day I mentioned to a colleague my suspicion that some aspirants for places, in their expressed determination to spend their lives as improverished doctors, were attempting to "do a snow job" on the admissions committee.

My friend grinned. "It's very worrying," he said, "for if what some of them say is true, we're in for an awful problem with an overdoctored Arctic!"

Chapter Three

Certainly many of the lecturers and professors at Scottish medical schools were men of deep Christian conviction. Mostly they were Presbyterians, stern humanitarians who imbued their students with the spirit of service. The needs of medicine and patients transcended all else.

I've seen the film *Chariots of Fire* twice, the second time, in 1985, out of sheer nostalgia. It seemed strange that a film should bring back so many thoughts of long ago.

The first time, I had gone because I was puzzled, wondering how an Oscar-winner could emerge from the story of two runners who long ago achieved the brief fame accorded to athletes. By today's standards they weren't even very fast. They led quite proper lives. There was a mild love interest in the film, I was told in advance, but it was all very prosaic and respectable. So why in this age of titillation and slick oversell did such a film get anywhere at all?

I had another reason for wanting to see it. In his time Eric Liddell was a hero to small Scots boys. Dubbed "the flying Scot," he was the fastest runner on earth. He had played rugby for Scotland. And I knew him. I daresay I boasted about that to other little boys. Now I wanted to see if the Eric Liddell of the film bore any resemblance to the Eric Liddell of my childhood.

I wasn't disappointed. The film protrayed a handsome athlete, a young man with a tremendous drive and sense of purpose. And I remembered that. I remembered the genial Eric Liddell who sat in our house talking to my father about his love for China and his determination to go back there, to follow in the steps of his father, a medical missionary. I remembered his preaching in our church and how I'd listened, spellbound. I also remember my mother's fears that my impressionable young mind might be influenced by this charming young man, that I might in turn follow in his footsteps.

Abrahams, Liddell's rival, despite his foreign parentage, unmistakably belonged to the English upper classes. Just as certainly Liddell was a middle-class Scot and a deeply religious one. Deeply religious Scots were once a national specialty. They were peculiar to the country, hardly understood by devout Englishmen who looked askance at their neighbours' cold northern Calvinism.

Liddell, however, was different. The young man I remember — and I met him only on a few occasions — left me with an impression of great warmth. He was a charming fellow, smiling easily, and I grinned as I saw the Eric Liddell of the film wink at the moonstruck schoolgirl in the front row of the congregation. My man would have done that out of sheer impishness.

Eric Liddell wasn't the kind of Scot that Robert Burns immortalized in "Holy Willie's Prayer," who could pray:

O Thou that in the Heavens does dwell,
Wha, as it pleases best Thysel,
Sends ane to Heaven an' ten to Hell
                              A' for Thy glory,
And no for onie guid or ill
                    They've done before Thee!
I bless and praise Thy matchless might,
When thousands Thou hast left in night,
That I am here before Thy sight,
                              For gifts an' grace
A burning and a shining light
                    To a' this place.

Burns knew a thing or two about the religiosity of the Scots of his time, of the narrow-mindedness and hypocrisy that often accompanied it. Religion has in many ways dominated Scottish history. It has dominated the thinking of countless Scots. It has produced strong men and devoted Christians who have fought to ease the lot of suffering humanity.

Religion drove Dr. David Livingstone, a Glasgow graduate of medicine, across the unknown continent of Africa, and it drove Eric Liddell back to China to help the toiling poor of that country. Liddell's love for all mankind, his gentleness and Christian humanity were, if not sophisticated, utterly genuine. Before seeing the film, I had not known the story of his refusal to run for Great Britain because the race was to be held on the Sabbath.

It must have taken great courage and complete conviction on Liddell's part to turn aside the appeals of that other charmer, Edward, Prince of Wales, and refuse to bow to any earthly prince in the face of his duty and commitment to a greater power. It was a very Scottish decision to make. It seemed apt, that at that interview with the assembled noblemen, who were no doubt meant to overcome yet appeal to Liddell, only the Duke of Sutherland, a fellow Scot by blood, yet English by up-bringing, understood his intransigence.

My Canadian friends have wondered about this Scottish religiosity, though some of it, for good or ill, has been transplanted to North America. "Why?" they've asked. "What was so wrong about running on a Sunday?"

Liddell, you see, would not just have been running on a Sunday. He was asked to run on the *Sabbath!* There is a subtle difference. The Sabbath is a day for rest, reflection and devotion. Sunday happens to be, to certain devout Scottish Protestants, the Sabbath. Its observance in many Scottish households of my childhood was complete and inviolable. Household duties, such as cooking and sewing, were forbidden. Regardless of my thoughts on the rigidity of such observances, it was Liddell's determination to stand by his principles that gripped me as I watched the film. It was his principles, too, that took him back to China.

Saving the Chinese from their "heathenism" was a great evangelical priority when I was a boy, and maps of the world were still half covered in red. We British all knew what that meant: we were masters of an Empire on which the sun never set. The Chinese, however, were held in special respect. They were worth saving.

There was no condescension, however, about Liddell's attitude to his chosen work as a missionary. He seemed to have a deep love for the Chinese people. Obviously he saw no conflict between his evangelical Christianity and his humanitarianism. He was a visionary.

A few years before the Second World War, with Eric Liddell in China and almost forgotten, I met another visionary. He was a fellow student, a Chinese boy a few years older than myself. One drizzly night we walked across a Glasgow square. My friend looked up at a monument, smiled and asked, "Why are Scottish monuments always erected for either missionaries or soldiers? In China our soldiers are bandits. They are hated. *Our* heroes are philosophers and scholars. Do you know that I have seen Scottish soldiers in Shanghai? And Scottish missionaries are everywhere. Do you know why Scottish soldiers are in China?"

I was too young to philosophize with him, but I've never forgotten his polite, enigmatic smile and the way he said, "Scottish soldiers are there because the white races have the machine gun. One day we Chinese, like you Scots, will begin to respect our soldiers. We will have the machine gun, too — and the whole world will tremble at the name of China.''

Eric Liddell did not live to see that vision appear, far away on the horizon. He died, a young man still, in a Japanese prison camp, of a brain tumour, his work unfinished.

Robert Louis Stevenson might have written for Liddell:

The morning drum-call on my eager ear,
Thrills unforgotten yet; the morning dew
Lies yet undried along my field of noon.
But now I pause at whiles in what I do,
And count the bell, and tremble lest I hear,
(My work untrimmed) The sunset gun too soon.

But Liddell, I think, would have said it had all been worth it. He had run the straight race.

I haven't seen much of Scotland in the last forty-five years. Nor could I describe myself as a religious man. But as I sat in the darkness of the cinema watching that story unfold, the Scottishness of my boyhood emerged from the shadow of the years, and I realized that try as I might, I had never been able to reject completely the religiosity of my youth.

Chapter Four

No one had said that our five years of study would be easy. Nor were they.

The first year was relatively painless. There were about 180 students in our year, a dozen or more being women students. Most of us were youngsters straight from high school. The study of botany, physics and chemistry posed no great hazard, and with one or two exceptions we gained entry to the second year of study.

The realities of our future were at once dramatically revealed to us when we walked into the anatomy dissecting room for the first time. Our nostrils were immediately assaulted by the pungent smell of formaldehyde, our minds drawn to our own brief mortality. For there on slabs, row upon row, lay corpses awaiting dissection.

Formaldehyde was used to preserve the bodies. However unpleasant, its smell disguises the odour of slowly deteriorating human flesh. It was a smell that would constantly be with us for the coming year, and for some of us it would linger forever.

Month after month we dissected nerves and blood vessels, memorizing their relative positions and their functions in the living being. Almost half of the year was spent in the physiology department studying the functioning of the body, the blood flow, and the working of the kidneys, lungs and other vital organs.

Second year was generally reckoned to be the most difficult year of all, surpassed only by the stress of the dreaded final examination at the end of the fifth year, when for several weeks, day after day, students aspiring to be qualified medical men and women would face the examiners.

In second year much memory work was involved. The tortuous course of nerves and blood vessels through the body must be known to perfection. The dissecting room with its sickly-sweet yet pungent smell in the summer heat disgusted some students, and a few resigned. Others saw their careers in medicine end with failure in the "second professional examination."

But a great vista of human discovery awaited the survivors. Third year was the first of three years of clinical study when we began to gain a knowledge of disease and how it can assault, invade, weaken and sometimes destroy our bodies.

Fifty years ago our profession had few effective remedies against illness. Aspirin was, and still is, one of our safest and most effective drugs, but even it has hazards. Digitalis was one of the few useful remedies for failing hearts, and tonics for general debility were very much in vogue. Perhaps those mixtures of *nux vomica* and traces of strychnine served a purpose, at least if accompanied by reassurance and encouragement from an understanding physician. But as medications they were generally useless.

Tuberculosis, though gradually vanishing, could infect — and kill — one family member after another. Children could develop a cold in the evening and waken paralyzed by poliomyelitis in the morning. Blood poisoning — acute septicaemia caused by the germ streptococcus invading even simple scratches received in household or garden work — could kill people within a few days. Smallpox still killed millions in the tropics. Today, smallpox seems to have been banished, and blood poisoning is so easily cured by the antibiotics.

Perhaps we have become complacent. Seemingly innocent organisms that live in relative harmony with their human hosts can become deadly if displaced to find feeding grounds in other parts of the human body. In Acquired Immune Deficiency Syndrome (or AIDS) where the death rate approached 100 per cent of those affected, simple fungi usually regarded as harmless cause dreadful complications in this fashion.

Forty years ago the practice of medicine was much less complicated than it is today. Our teachers were mostly generalists — general surgeons, physicians and obstetricians. The superspecialist was a rarity. A few of our teachers were developing specialized interests, but heart surgeons were as yet unheard of, as were surgeons specializing in injuries of the hand or neonatologists with special interest in the well-being of the newborn, and the many other subspecialists of today.

The women students, much in the minority, were given no favours; neither were they discouraged. They might be subjected to bawdy humour by some of the teachers, but discrimination was unusual, and in this respect medicine was more enlightened than some of its sister professions. Still, a dozen or so women in a class of nearly two hundred was a far cry from the often 50 per cent of women medical students in classes of the 1980s. Some of our work was heartbreaking, and some revolting, but the women students shared it.

The septic wards were a feature of those times. Almost always they were situated in hospital basements. The stench was terrible, despite all efforts to keep the places ventilated. All kinds of dreadful injuries and infections were treated there: wounds, abscesses and burns that refused to heal, discharging foul pus for months on end.

Burns were very liable to become first infected and then septic, despite impeccable nursing care. They could take many months to heal, and extensive burns could kill, after causing the patient a tortured existence. The septic wards have long gone, thank God.

What cures there were in those miserable places were seldom attributable to scientific medical treatment. They were, rather, the result of devoted nursing. The septic wards seemed to draw to them excellent nurses, attractive young women immaculate in their uniforms, working day after day in abominable stench and misery, seeing suffering that must have been almost unequalled in civilized society of the times. Yet they were caring and encouraging, and always, it seemed, despite their tragic surroundings, cheerful. They put us, in our brief instructional sessions, to shame.

Despite the lack of scientific therapy, scientific diagnosis was extremely important, for research was beginning to prove its worth. In the 1930s, our profession was on the brink of great discoveries and enormous advances.

Clinical observation was still considered to be an important part of our education. Dr. Sam Cameron, professor and head of the department of obstetrics, was not beyond pressing home the value of such observation. Dr. Cameron was a big, jovial man. With hands like hams, Sam Cameron was nevertheless noted for performing surgery of gentle, deft sureness.

He was lecturing to a small group on the importance of the early recognition of diabetes in pregnancy. The one woman in the group was Janet Grant, the girl I would later marry.

"Now, how would you recognize the presence of sugar in the urine?" he asked his listeners.

"Fehling's test, sir," replied one student immediately.

"Oh! There's one easier than that," replied the professor.

"Benedict's test, sir?"

"No. Easier than that, even. Taste. Ye taste the urine. Ye see," said

Dr. Cameron, dipping his forefinger into a beaker full of urine and licking appreciatively, "it's very easy. Here you try it, Grainger. And now you, MacTavish. And of course, we mustn't forget the ladies. You try it, Miss Grant."

Years later, Janet told me how, blushing to the roots of her auburn hair, she tried to decline Professor Cameron's invitation, but finally she dipped a finger into the revolting fluid and performed the test.

Dr. Cameron shook his head, more in sorrow than in anger. "Ye see," he said, "you're not developing your sense of observation at all, any of you. If you'd been observant, you'd have seen me dip my index finger in the urine. But it was my middle finger I licked. You'll all have to do better than that!" he concluded, with a mischievous grin.

Chapter Five

Medical students used to have a reputation for being pretty wild. It did not apply to my generation. We were a pretty earnest lot, too young, too close to the Calvinistic upbringing imposed upon us by Scottish tradition to be otherwise. Gaining our degrees, for most of us, surpassed all other desires. "Getting on in life" seemed to be our clarion call.

Some fellows occasionally drank too much, but drinking was unusual, and sexual adventures were generally inhibited by the hazards attendant on them. There was more talk than action. The world, for a few years at least, seemed a secure place for those who saw the road ahead.

But that view was being clouded in the 1930s. Fascism was on the march, barely twenty years after the end of the Great War in which millions of the Allies' youngest and brightest men had been slaughtered. The fear of war infected our parents. Photographs of handsome lads who had been killed in action hung in every Scottish sitting room, it seemed — "That's my uncle Alex — he was killed at Ypres — and that's my brother Jim, killed on the Somme."

My father often talked of his six cousins, the McKenzie boys: "Not one of them under six feet, five of them in the Seaforth Highlanders and one at sea. Not one alive at the end of the War." It was no wonder that our parents' faces saddened as they spoke of war.

But whatever the future held for us, the study of medicine was all important. Nothing must stand in the way. We were young, impressionable and face-to-face with disease and suffering for the first time in our lives. We were only beginning to develop the protective skin of feigned unconcern at tragedy that often seemed essential to our survival as medical men and women.

Not surprisingly, a great many of us at one time or another suffered temporarily from the imagined symptoms of a fatal disease. Cancer was, and still is, the most prevalent terminal illness that medical students imagine they have developed.

My own "case" was brought on by one of our professors giving a lecture on sarcoma of bone — a particularly vile type of cancer. Professor Burton tended to illustrate his notes with dramatic descriptions of cases he had seen.

"In this particular instance," he told us, "the first evidence of sarcoma was when this student collapsed on the very steps of the university. Quite unknown to him, healthy bone in his thigh had been replaced by cancerous tissue. He had suffered a pathological fracture of the femur. His diseased leg simply broke under him."

Having let this picture sink in, he went on: "Of course, we amputated his leg, but there was really nothing we could do. It should be remembered that bone sarcoma may follow an injury. This student had received, nine months before, a heavy, ponderous blow on the thigh. It was a great pity," he concluded, "for he was an extremely bright young man with a splendid future ahead of him."

Now I wasn't an extremely bright young man and I didn't see too far into the future, but it just so happened that on the previous Saturday I had received a heavy, ponderous blow on my right thigh.

I was a rugby football player, not a brilliant one either, but useful, which is about the only accolade bestowed upon me. I usually played as a scrum-half, whose function it is to grab the ball from beneath the feet of sixteen shoving, swearing men and throw it out to the fleet of foot. In doing so, he is often charged by large men from the opposing team who, if they can, fall upon him with heavy, ponderous force. That is what had happened to me two days previously.

My thigh was still sore from Saturday's game, and for the next nine months it was very much on my mind. On more than one occasion I might have been seen measuring the circumference of my upper legs with great concentration.

The power of suggestion for good or evil is enormous and no doctor should ever forget that when talking to patients. A friend who later became a neurologist told me how at the age of twenty-one he had been told to stand before the class while he was demonstrated as the typical candidate for multiple sclerosis, then as now an incurable disease of the central nervous system.

"For fifteen years," my friend told me, "I couldn't get that lecture out of my head. 'Observe his build,' the lecturer had intoned. 'Note the colour of his eyes, the delicate complexion.' Although I became a neurologist myself later on, and knew the fellow's theories were rubbish, I still had that nagging fear at the back of my mind."

Many of the patients we studied as we walked the wards were middle-aged or elderly. A person of sixty seemed to a very young man to have one foot in the grave anyway, so we could accept the inevitability of death in many cases of illness in older people. But the young, too, died and often tragically. We students then saw death in the young much oftener than we do today and we accepted its inevitability. We had to.

Fiona McIntosh was very beautiful, red-haired, blue-eyed and exquisitely shapely, a year or two older than myself and a graduate of the university. She was a Highland girl, a schoolteacher. Growing up in the clear air of Sutherland, she had not acquired immunity to the infectious diseases that plagued such young people who came to work in the smog and crowded conditions of the cities. And now, she was a patient.

I was in my fourth year of study and Fiona had been allocated to me, my duties being to take a concise history of her illness, observe and record her progress.

Several months previously she had developed a seemingly simple sore throat, but three weeks later she began to complain of painful and swollen joints. She became feverish and unable to continue at her work. Then her heart became affected, failing to pump properly. The heart valves became encrusted with infective vegetations, and she was admitted to hospital with the diagnosis of subacute bacterial endocarditis. Fiona had rheumatic fever. Thankfully, it is a disease we seldom see today, but it was all too common then, and deadly. Remember, the antibiotics were a decade away.

Fiona was a sweet thing, uncomplaining and grateful for little kindnesses shown her by nurses and doctors. Her parents, humble folk who were devoted to her, lived too far away to visit often, and feeling sorry for her, I took to sitting beside her in my spare time.

I knew she looked forward to my vists and they were a pleasure for me, with her welcoming smile, her beauty enhanced by the flush on her cheeks. But that flush proclaimed a low fever and steady deterioration in her condition.

I had been looking after her for perhaps two months when Dr. Robert

Dunkeld summoned me to his office. Dr. Dunkeld was more direct than fatherly and he came straight to the point.

"Mr. Gibson, you have been seeing a good deal of Miss McIntosh."

"Yes, sir. She's my patient,"

"But you haven't been confining yourself altogether to your duties, have you? You spend a lot of time with her."

"Sir, I feel sorry for her."

"Do you have a sweetheart, Gibson?"

"No, sir."

"Miss McIntosh is very beautiful. Feeling sorry for such a beautiful young woman could be the first step towards caring for her. Gibson, you will not be working in that ward tomorrow. You will be given another patient elsewhere. You are not to visit Miss McIntosh again. That is an order," said the professor with military directness.

"I'm not in love with her, sir," I protested.

Dr. Dunkeld rose to his feet.

"Perhaps not," he said, "but you must not take the chance of falling in love with her. She is dying. It may be months, or if she's lucky, a few years. You must not be allowed to saddle yourself with an invalid. You have a career to think of. That is all. Good day to you."

Weeks later I went back to the ward. Fiona McIntosh had gone to a small hospital near her home in the Highlands, her years of study at university spent for naught, her parents' sacrifice and dreams destroyed.

She deserved better.

Robert Burns, one cold November morning, when plowing on his Ayrshire farm, destroyed the nest of a field mouse. Watching the tiny creature run way, its little world in ruins, prompted him to write his poem "To a Mouse."

It ends:

But Mousie, thou art no thy lane,
In proving foresight may be vain:
The best-laid schemes o' mice an' men
     Gang aft agley,
An' lea'e us nought but grief an' pain,
     For promis'd joy!

Still thou art blest, compar'd wi' me!
The present only toucheth thee:
But och! I backward cast my e'e,
                              On prospects drear!
An' forward, tho' I canna see,
                              I guess an' fear!

Chapter Six

I sometimes think that in the practice of medicine today we don't look at things the way we used to. Diagnosis, once an art, has become a science. Nowadays we listen to our patients' stories, often rather perfunctorily, and carry out competent enough examinations. Then we take a sample of blood and one of urine, feed them into a computerized laboratory system, and out come the results, all neatly ticketed on a form. Usually the answers are correct.

Of course, we *should* use computers and every piece of scientific technology we can, but we should not neglect the training of our powers of observation. We depend too much on expensive and sometimes unnecessary laboratory tests. We might do well, to some extent, to return to the days of "the elegant diagnosis," when, lacking today's advanced techniques, doctors had to rely on their observational senses. We learned to listen to the nuances of a patient's story and put two and two together.

In making a diagnosis we can learn much by simple means: the colour and consistency of a patient's sputum, or urine, or the patient's appearance. Even as our patients come into our consulting rooms our diagnostic sense can be at work: Does the patient's face portray anxiety, aggression? Is it grey in colour, or too florid? Is he or she carefully or carelessly dressed? Has there been an exaggerated, unexpected or unusual change in the mode of dress or behaviour? Has there been a loss or gain of weight? Even the eyes can tell a great deal, from jaundice to an overactive thyroid. The list of clues is almost endless.

Conan Doyle fashioned Sherlock Holmes after his old tutor in medicine at the University of Edinburgh. Lacking today's laboratory tests, the old-time clinicians became expert observers. Conan Doyle's professor was a master of the elegant diagnosis, and his powers of observation were acutely developed. He could usher a patient into his study and within minutes, without a word being spoken, astound both patient and students by correctly stating the sufferer's type of work, and from that, by deduction, his probable illness.

On one occasion he silently looked at a newcomer, then said that not only was he an ex-soldier, but a regimental piper, and a deserter. All this, from noting the man's walk and stance. He had the military swagger that pipers often develop, and he tried to hide his wrist on which was branded the letter D, the military custom of the time with soldiers who sought greener pastures. He had at one time been branded a deserter.

In the 1930s some of our teachers carried on this deductive tradition. The middle-aged coal miner could be identified by thin scars of coal dust ingrained in his back, and extra attention would be paid to the possibility of lung disease. Since people in certain types of work tended to develop specific illnesses, a well-developed sense of observation and deduction was a skill worth having.

I was not trying to emulate the great detective when, in a ward of the Western Infirmary, Glasgow, long ago, I was called to look at three casualties, just admitted. I was not called to see them because of my acknowledged brilliance; I was a mere student and usually beneath the notice of everybody, but I was the only man in the place wearing a white coat. And because the patients were making an awful noise.

I was examining patients on the other side of the ward and minding my own business when Sister Munro came for me. In North America she'd be called a nursing supervisor, but in Scotland, although the religious nursing orders had long gone, the old title was retained. While carrying out my duties I was trying to hear above the moans and groans of the frightened newcomers. Sister came to my side.

I rather liked Sister. She ran an efficient ward. The nurses weren't afraid of her, and indeed she'd been seen giggling with a couple of probationers once or twice. This was a bit unusual. Sisters tended to be middle-aged spinsters who lived for their vocation, and were martinets, not to be taken lightly. It was said, with some justification, that one or two of them bossed their chiefs around like hired help.

But not Sister Munro. At thirty-five or so she was rather a "looker," and why someone had never snatched her up must remain a mystery. She was dark and shapely, and met with the general approval, visual and otherwise, of my classmates. The patients respected her, and she obviously cared for them. The ward, even with her velvet-glove technique of management, worked well.

Would I go and look at these three men who'd just been brought in, she asked. There were making a fearful noise, upsetting everyone and, poor souls, they couldn't speak any English. If I just went over and looked, it might help. The surgical resident was in the operating theatre and other patients thought the men were being neglected. So did they, and if I went over in my white coat it would look official and everyone would cool down. It was good psychology, spoiled a little for me by her remark that the resident would find out what was wrong when he'd finished operating. Sister Munro implied that my assistance would be appreciated, but minimal.

The patients were three East Indian seamen who had fallen into the hold of a Clan liner in Glasgow docks. They were terrified, and had one word of English between them: "yes," which became "*yes, yes, yes*" for emphasis. They had been examined by someone in the casualty department and sent upstairs accompanied by a ship's officer who had given some details of the case and departed. Two of them seemed to me more voluble than damaged, but the third man was obviously in pain. His normally brown face had turned that chalky grey colour so indicative of trouble in dark-skinned people. Briefly, I went from one to the other. The two men who were causing most of the trouble ceased their wailing when I examined their limbs and reflexes, watching me with anxious, intense interest. The third patient, however, when I turned his bed clothes down, only rolled the whites of his eyes at me and moaned.

"There's something really wrong here," I thought as I commenced my examination. He looked shocked, his pulse was unsteady and he groaned quietly as I touched him, however gently. Then there it was. I could see the trouble before I even palpated his abdomen. Just above the pubic bones the abdomen was slightly swollen. Not very noticeable, but when I examined him gently, he drew his head back and twisted his neck from one side to the other. He was obviously in acute discomfort.

Drawing the blankets over him, I turned to Sister. She stood there in her dark blue uniform with the white apron, hands clasped in front of her. Two of her nurses stood beside her, silently watching.

"He's got an acute retention of urine, Sister. He can't pass his water."

"Now, how would you know that, I'd like to know," she said. "His abdomen isn't distended, as far as I could see!"

"Well, that's it," I replied. "He needs to have his bladder emptied. Look, Sister, they fell into the hold, didn't they? So this chap could have an injury to his spine, couldn't he? And so he could have a paralysis of his bladder."

"My goodness," said Sister, looking at me for the first time as if

I might really be quite an intelligent fellow, "you could be right! If only we could talk to him!"

"Sister, allow me." Turning to the patient, I said in my best professional manner, "*Panee lao.*" The effect was magical. There was a sudden babble of high-toned, singsong voices. All three of them spoke to me at once.

"*Panee lao,* Sahib! *Panee lao.*"

"Yes, yes, yes. *Panee lao,* Sahib."

"You see," I said to an astounded Sister and her goggle-eyed companions. "He needs his water brought. Someone should pass a catheter."

Bowing slightly to the ladies, I made my way back to my patients, sensing, rather than knowing, that six pairs of eyes were watching my stately progress across the ward floor.

The next morning the ward was its usual quiet, subdued, well-ordered self — until I arrived. Then there was uproar. Three East Indian seamen at the tops of their voices hailed me like a long lost brother from the far end of the ward. "Sahib! Sahib! Sahib! Yes, yes, Sahib!"

Following the example of my previous chief, Dr. MacIntyre, who every morning shook hands with recent arrivals to his wards — a gesture of courtesy that seldom escaped notice — I made my way to their beds, shook hands with all three, and duly took note of the catheter leading from my stricken friend's bladder to a glass container on the ward floor, I expressed my delight at this happier state of affairs, but since they were all smiles and all talking at once, I didn't linger, and found something useful to do elsewhere. The quiet atmosphere of the ward was deteriorating rapidly and I could see that Sister was a little disturbed. But she was a kind creature and felt compassion for the poor unfortunates far from home. She even smiled at me as I discreetly withdrew.

The next morning it began all over again, but Sister was waiting for me.

"Look," she said, "it's all very well, but for goodness' sake go and tell those men they must not shout at you the minute you walk in here. I'm sorry for them. But you go and tell them I just can't have it. I know it's great for them to be able to speak to you in their own language, but the noise —"

I interrupted her. "Sister," I said, "I don't know their language!"

"But the other night...you were all speaking to one another like natives."

"Sister, *they* were all speaking like natives," I replied. "I don't know their language. But I do know my Kipling," and I recited:

It was Din! Din! Din!
'Ere's a beggar with a bullet through 'is spleen;
  'E's chawin' up the ground,
  An' 'e's kickin' all around:
For Gawd's sake git the water, Gunga Din!...
  Water, git it! *Panee lao!*
You squidgy-nosed old idol, Gunga Din.

I paused. *"Panee lao* — fetch water fast. It was easy, Sister — Gunga Din."

She stood there, those lovely eyes of hers on my face, and said, "Well, I'll be damned. You fake."

Her arm was slowly raised. Her finger pointed into the distance behind me. "Outside," she said, "and stay out."

"Sister, my patients..." I pleaded.

"Outside," she said again. "Your patients will survive without you. This ward will not survive *with* you. There are quite able people who can relieve you of your responsibilities. Outside! I'll send for you when they're moved."

"Sister..."

Beautiful women are often deceptive. They can be formidable and even ruthless. All she did was keep pointing at the door behind me.

"Out you go."

It sometimes doesn't pay to be helpful *or* observant.

Chapter Seven

I had missed the early commuter train for Glasgow and the first of the morning's lectures. I had slept in. I simply couldn't afford being absent from the second lecture.

Joining me in my desperate rush to the station to board the next train was John Gibb, a crony of mine and a fellow student.

The conductor had just waved his red flag, blown his whistle and boarded the guard's van. The train was gliding forward as we wrenched open a door and tumbled into a compartment, followed by shouted invective from the guard. His remarks would not have endeared him to our minister.

Even with a rush from Glasgow's Central Station and good luck in finding a tramcar bound for the university, we were going to be late for Dr. Joseph McLuhan's lecture.

I had a number of reasons for not wishing to miss Dr. McLuhan's lecture, not the least of them being the doctor himself.

In those days there was none of the easy camaraderie between faculty and students that exists today. Lecturers and professors were, if not gods, the next best thing; with few exceptions they expected their fair due in the way of reverence from their juniors. They certainly expected attendance at their classes, having been known to lock doors in the face of latecomers and to take names.

Dr. McLuhan was quite a democrat compared with some of his colleagues, but he had intimated that he expected a full attendance at *this* particular lecture.

I looked upon him with wary respect. He could be a poker-faced humourist and tormentor, and ever since I had joined the clinic in which he lectured, I'd had a running battle with him.

He would keep referring to me as "the lotus-eater of the year," a quite inaccurate judgement, for I was a diligent and earnest student. I had to be, just to keep abreast of the work.

Dr. McLuhan was in his early fifties, a tall, well-built fellow with the face of a boxer, and so exquisitely tailored that some of the girls declared that he wore corsets. He certainly wore two medical hats, one as a pioneer in haematology — the study of blood diseases — the other in a much older field of endeavour: the treatment of venereal disease. He was also an excellent lecturer. This morning his subject was to be a routine but important discussion of urinary problems.

The problem for Gibb and myself was how to insinuate ourselves into the class during the lecture without attracting attention. Easy. Having reached the university, we'd slip up the back stairs, edge open the back door of the lecture hall and slip into the back bench. It had been done before, and with over a hundred listeners hanging on to his every word, McLuhan would never notice us.

Our plan seemed faultless. Inch by inch we opened the door. It hardly even creaked. But unfortunately the back bench was already full of other latecomers. Grudgingly they made room for us and there was some scuffling of feet — but for which there might have been none of the trouble that ensued.

"Give me one more substance that will acidify the urine," McLuhan was saying, pausing just long enough to cast a cold glance in our direction.

"Ascorbic acid, sir," someone volunteered.

"Correct. And another, please!"

So it went on. Gradually, it seemed to me, various members of the class had identified every substance that might maintain an acid balance in a patient's urine, but Dr. McLuhan, poker-faced, kept on.

"One more, please. There *must* be one more!"

It was then that the trouble began. The women students, by tradition, occupied the two front rows of the lecture hall. There wasn't any easy camaraderie in class between the sexes either in those days.

Up piped one of the ladies questioningly, "Dilute nitric acid, sir?"

Now, nitric acid has caustic properties that can take the lining off a steel pipe, and the possibilities of such a chemical, even greatly diluted, coursing through one's urinary system intrigued me.

There was silence in the class. Dr. McLuhan appeared to have gone into a state of trance and I whispered to Gibb, "John, how would you like to waken up one morning to find your John Tom corroded away?"

Gibb stood over six feet in height, weighed more than two hundred pounds, and his gargantuan guffaw alarmed me and roused our lecturer from his reverie. Suddenly he looked towards us. I favoured my companion with a glance that implied distance and disdain, if not disgust.

"Stand up!"

Gibb rose to his feet.

"Not you. YOU!"

Dr. McLuhan was looking unwaveringly towards me, and reluctantly I stood.

My observation had been heard and passed along the back bench. There was some tittering.

"You appear, Gibson," said the doctor, "to have cast a pearl of wit — amongst swine," he added, looking witheringly at the occupants of the back row. "I feel sure you would not deny us all the benefits of your witticism."

"No, sir, I'd rather not, if you don't mind."

"Ah! But I do mind. It's very unfair. The ladies," he said with extra-sensory perception, "would, I feel sure, be interested."

"Sir, I don't think so."

Demure faces in the front row were turned towards me. My discomfiture increased with every passing second.

"But you must let me be the judge of that. Gibson, you have the floor."

"Thank you, sir, no sir."

Dr. McLuhan strolled up the steep steps of the lecture theatre and stood beside me.

"Well, so you refuse to share your wisdom with us?"

"It's not wisdom, sir."

"I feel sure of that. But since you refuse my orders, you must come and sit beside the girls."

Taking me firmly by the arm, our instructor led me down to the front row and deposited me in the middle of the first row of women students.

The lecture proceeded uneventfully. Gibb was waiting for me outside the lecture room. Our fellow students had dispersed and we were alone in the long hospital corridor.

Suddenly a hand was placed on my shoulder.

It was Dr. McLuhan.

"Ah well," he said, "anything to brighten up a dull morning. But now tell me what you said."

So I told him.

"Very funny," he remarked. "Oh! Very funny," and made to move ahead of us when Gibb put his foot in it all over again.

"Oh, sir," he said, "Gibson and I would like to come to Black Street next term to do our VD. Would that be all right?"

Black Street was known to every doctor, nurse and health worker in the city. It was the clinical teaching and treatment centre for venereal disease, and Dr. McLuhan was one of the supervising physicians.

"I'd have to think about that," replied our lecturer. "And I'll let you know," he added as he walked rapidly past us.

He'd just reached the top of the stairs when a group of off-duty nurses fluttered up them, chattering and smiling, each one of them prettier than the other and all of them known to us.

They were just passing Dr. McLuhan when he turned sharply towards the two of us and pointed at me, silencing the girls.

"Oh, Gibson," he bellowed, "I've thought about it. Just come and see me at Black Street any time."

Chapter Eight

Nineteen thirty-nine saw our final year of study. It was a momentous one, yet our personal problems and decisions hardly mattered, for Europe was moving inexorably towards war.

The threat of war seemed only to harden our resolve as students to pass the finals before the blow fell. The examinations lasted for about two weeks, encompassing all that we had learned, and were both written and oral.

The finals are ordeals fraught with tension. The prospect drove many of us to spend long hours in study, working into the early hours of the morning, snatching a few hours of sleep, then attending classes where we hoped to pick up some morsel of information about a new treatment, or a pointer towards making a diagnosis in some disease, that rumour whispered would appear as a question in "the writtens."

It was a momentous year for me in other respects. I met the woman who later became my wife. Janet Grant, petite, very pretty and gloriously auburn-haired, was a classmate.

For two years, we students had been scattered across the city in various hospitals and so it was difficult to have easy contact with one another. A few months before our finals, however, Janet and I were thrown together in a small group session by the alphabetical selection of names, and very soon we found ourselves studying together.

A two-penny tramcar ride could take us twenty miles away from the grime of the city to the bonnie banks of Loch Lomond, where I could have imagined nothing more pleasurable than to study with Janet Grant as a companion. For all her femininity I found a young woman filled with as grim a determination as my own to succeed in her profession.

The crucial month of September drew nearer. Anxiously, frantically and sometimes despairingly, students covered and re-covered the ground. While the world watched events with sinking hearts as Hitler invaded Poland, most of us final-year people thought only of the examinations ahead. Most but not all, for as war was declared and the examinations began, some of our classmates, reservists in the forces, were already in uniform. Some would live for only a few brief months.

My friend Alexander McArthur, formerly a ship's captain, extra-master mariner and officer of the Royal Naval Reserve, was such a one. In his middle thirties, he had invested his savings to fulfil his lifelong ambition of becoming a doctor. He had had a faultless passage through medical school until September 1939, when he failed in one crucial subject. Relentlessly he was recalled to the navy, not as a surgeon but as a deck officer. We kept writing to one another until within the year no further letters arrived. Alex had been killed in action.

When the first day of the finals arrived, few of us thought much farther ahead than the next two weeks. The written examinations came first, and as we were called we went into the university's huge, grey Bute Hall and hurried to our allotted desks. For some, not a moment must be lost. Pens were seized, there was a swift scrutiny of the questions, and they were off in a fury of writing. Others perused the examination paper, stared into space in concentration, then wrote. Some poor souls decided to call it a day and quietly left the hall.

I seemed to write with snail-like speed and became alarmed when, my writing paper scantily filled, I saw people rise and ask for more.

Following one examination I met a fellow who seemed to possess a flying pen, and grumpily I commented on the number of sheets of paper he had used. Had I been wiser I'd have kept my remarks to myself. His response did nothing for my peace of mind.

"Oh yes," he said loftily, "but then I expect I shall get a distinction. The questions were an absolute cinch for me."

The oral examinations were another kind of ordeal altogether. Day after day we met the examiners, usually two of them together, one of them from another university. They could be kindly or cold, polite, brusque or even hostile. Some had a reputation for testiness or for holding pet theories about their pet diseases (in which case great diplomacy was called for) and some had fearsome reputations, probably quite unjustly acquired. Under their watchful eyes we examined patients and made diagnoses, or peered into glass jars containing age-old specimens of human tissue from the pathology department and made guesses.

But all things come to an end and during the next two to three weeks we retired, mentally exhausted, to await the results.

When we sat our finals we probably knew more of the broad spectrum of medicine than we would ever know again, for postgraduate examinations would be concerned only with the various specialties of our craft.

Within the month the results were posted on the university notice board. There would be a crush of students jostling and struggling to read the names, so, determined not to have witnesses to what might be humiliation, I let an hour or two pass before I went near the place.

Groups of my classmates were still standing around. Some were walking away, their grim faces proclaiming their news.

But I had passed and so had Janet Grant. The fellow who had so grandly told me he had expected a distinction failed and so had many others, despite the rumour that with war having been declared, we'd all be "shoved through."

The next day, in a slightly euphoric mood, I decided to visit my old ward. I was wearing my best suit.

"What will it be," I thought as I climbed the stairs to the hospital corridor. "Shall I call myself Dr. W.M. Gibson, or Dr. William M. Gibson, or Dr. W. Morrison Gibson?"

I was still pondering the relative suitability of these lofty choices as I approached the closed ward doors. They opened suddenly when I was a dozen or so yards away, and who should stroll towards me, impeccably tailored as ever, but my old adversary, Dr. Joseph McLuhan.

My first thought was, "Just you wait, McLuhan — I'll be wearing a suit like that one day." But a more generous mood prevailed as I anticipated his greeting.

"Congratulations!" he'd say. "Well done, Gibson — a brother physician — one of this great priesthood dedicated to..."

But he didn't seem to see me. His eyes seemed to be fixed on something at the far end of the corridor, and then, just as he passed me, he murmured, as if to himself, "Well, blow me over. We've given him his licence to kill!"

Chapter Nine

Nineteen thirty-nine had been a strange year. The war clouds did not dispel the warmth of that beautiful summer, nor the pressures of work the enjoyment of films like *The Citadel* with Robert Donat as the doctor-hero, *The Lives of a Bengal Lancer* — an epic of Imperial hocus-pocus — nor the lilting music of *The Great Waltz* with the most glamorous of sopranos, Miliza Korjus playing the part of the femme fatale.

I had met the girl I would marry and I seemed to spend a good deal of my time cheerfully whistling the film's theme-song: "One Morning in May."

And yet we were at war in October and I was unemployed.

Hospitals had been evacuated, wards closed for everyday use as they were prepared for air raid and battle casualties. But there were neither air raids nor casualties. It was the calm before the awful storm, but to Britishers it was the phony war, and many of my classmates, like myself, were its casualties in a different way. We weren't wanted.

Doctors who had spent a year or more as medical residents in hospital, and who should have been moving into practice, were refused permission to leave their posts. Their skills, it was thought, would shortly be needed. Consequently, newly graduated physicians who should have been replacing them were without work, and any kind of commitment to the forces rendered a man almost unemployable. Hospital chiefs did not want to engage young men who could be called up at a moment's notice, leaving wards without medical help.

Eventually I found work as an assistant in general practice in a small Lancashire mill town, a grim, grimy place, cheered only by the warmth of its people. In the few months I stayed there, if I learned nothing about academic medicine I learned a great deal about life. I learned to make quick decisions, for having dealt with the morning surgery — as office sessions are called in Britain — where patients waited stolidly in the corridor that served as a waiting room, or outside in the rain for "consultations" that lasted a minute or two, there were the day's house calls to deal with. There might be twenty or thirty of those.

The variety of illness was bewildering and the challenge immense for such a newly qualified man. Bronchitis abounded, often caused by a lifetime of exposure to the unhealthy atmosphere of the cotton mills and the soot that belched continuously from their tall chimneys. On one windy day from the hillside above the town I counted seventeen of them, all pouring out the soot that on calm and foggy days would fall like snow into the valley.

And there were other illnesses. Cancer was commonplace, and dying people spent their last days in the wretchedness of their tiny, damp back-to-back houses, and they had to be visited. In terms of cold science nothing was accomplished by such visits, but it would be a hard or insensitive man who could not feel the gratitude that was shown and perhaps the comfort that was given.

Children became ill with the infectious diseases that were rife. Fortunately many of them, such as diptheria, tuberculosis and scarlet fever, have all but vanished, but forty years ago they would spread from house to house like wildfire, bringing disaster and grief in the end.

It was not an easy life but it was a rewarding, challenging one, and I would not have missed it for worlds. It was medicine in the raw, perhaps, and had little to do with the university's "grove of academe," but it was a splendid apprenticeship.

In that small town the houses were jammed together, street by street, and I could do five or six house calls in an hour. The evening surgeries began at 5 P.M. and went on until the last patient had been seen, usually about 8 P.M. Nighttime emergency calls were always the assistant's business.

There was nothing unusual about that practice. There must have been hundreds of us, especially in the industrial north. Perhaps employers regarded us young fellows as birds-of-passage anyway, and that we should work hard for our £5 15s per week.

Later on I was privileged to work for a month or two with two family doctors who conducted their practice on a different level. There were conferences each morning about patients and the house calls to be done that day. Specialists were consulted about worrying cases, and patients, however poor, were treated with competence and compassion.

I began to see the challenge of general practice and I learned the real value of the doctor's visit. The house call is a disappearing part of general practice and in many ways its loss is regrettable.

Today we live in litigious times. Perhaps doctors are justified in referring night calls and emergencies to hospitals. By assessing patients' illnesses in their homes without the benefit of every piece of emergency equipment that may be necessary, doctors are perhaps exposing themselves to charges of malpractice. The costs of litigation are rising astronomically, but the house calls of years ago often created a lasting bond of trust between doctors and their patients. There was an intimacy about such occasions. Patients seeing ''their own doctor'' in their own homes tended to forgive oversights on the part of their physicians.

Nowadays sick people sometimes have to leave the comfort of their beds and wait in hospital emergency rooms or all-night clinics, occasionally for long periods, to see a doctor. And if the doctor is busy and impersonal, there can be a loss of that old and maybe overpraised relationship.

House calls, if worthwhile, were a useful and rewarding part of a general practitioner's life, and I'm not sure that their disappearance has benefited anyone, including my profession.

But in the summer of 1940 I suddenly realized that for the foreseeable future they wouldn't be of any concern to me.

The war had begun in earnest and I was called up.

Chapter Ten

The regiment to which I was sent was officered almost exclusively by Englishmen. Several of my new companions in the headquarters mess, of which I was to be a member for a year, were serving officers of the regular army. Others were retired officers who had been recalled from the reserve. They were Sandhurst graduates and had studied at the Royal Military Academy for gunnery officers at Woolwich, near London. This establishment they referred to fondly, if offhandedly, as Shop.

They were the products of public schools (as English private schools for the upper classes are called) and there wasn't a single bluff-spoken north countryman among them. They were southerners to a man, courteous and well spoken — most of the time. There were rare occasions when their language was lurid. They were masters of understatement who considered open displays of patriotic sentiment either amusing or ill-mannered. Patriotism was something they accepted as naturally as they did their right as gentlemen to lead the rest.

On the rare occasions that I saw Janet during that year, I used to tell her that had the colonel ordered them to advance against the enemy, canes in hand, they would have done so without question. One or two of them might have fumbled as they put their silk handkerchiefs properly into their tunic sleeves, but that would have been all. Many years later it seems as vivid an impression as ever.

Several of them had recently returned to Britain after years of service in India. They lived for horses, and were revolted by the idea of having to haul cannon behind motor vehicles. They were horse gunners, and eyed the rest of military mankind with a certain disdain, though the Guards and some of the British and Indian cavalry regiments met with their approval. Their stories of Afghan ways of dealing with prisoners would have furnished Freud with much material for further study.

"We were operating on the northwest frontier," said the colonel one night when the mess was quiet. The quartermaster and he were reminiscing about old times in India. I was their audience.

"The local tribes had got out of hand. They were raiding villages across the border in India, so it was decided that we should slap them sharply on the wrist for being naughty. I commanded a battery of mountain guns in those days and we followed the infantry, our job being to dislodge the blighters from any shelter they might find.

"Our advance party of Sikhs went ahead of the main body, and bless me if these damned Pathans didn't ambush them in a gully. They got every last man of them, too. By the time our main body arrived, the raiders had gone, but not before carrying out their little ritual. They'd beheaded the lot! Then they cut their penises off and put them in their victims' mouths as a gesture of contempt.

"When I arrived with the guns, all lickety-spit and tickety-boo, there were all these corpses lying about with their owners' turbaned heads perched on rocks and their cocks stuck in their mouths.

"It was," said the colonel mildly, turning to me and fingering his tie, "just a little bit off-putting, don't y' know, Doc."

The returnees did not like what they saw at home. The army was changed — to them, almost literally beyond recognition — with the imposition of a new uniform called battle dress. They detested it and the politicians who were, in their opinion, its innovators. Most of them were conservatives in every sense of the word, and they thought the Germans were a damned and graceless lot, with all their tanks and mechanical devices.

Motorcars were for going up to London in; their use for killing people was ungentlemanly. Not that these men minded killing people. That was their trade, and on the northwest borders of India they had given as good as they got. But the Germans, as Dick West, the adjutant, said, were "just going to make this war look like a bloody great industrial accident."

The horse gunners wore their long, distinctive riding tunics with a certain panache. The rest of us sported regulation uniform as worn by lesser breeds.

The regimental second-in-command, a major, was not a horse gunner. He was a London barrister and, I was told, a very successful one. He was an interesting man, with manners as impeccably cold as his intellect. Handsome, tall, courtly, correct and unsmiling, he would have been a formidable opponent in a court of law. He struck me as the kind of

50

man whose forte would be prosecution rather than defence, and the rows of decorations and campaign ribbons on his uniform enhanced that impression and testified to his distinction as a soldier in the First World War.

He was the first man to appear in the mess wearing battle dress, and he looked well in it. The colonel never wore it in the year I was with them. "Those damned pyjamas," he used to snort. There were occasional touches of unexpected raffishness about the colonel that did not sit well with the major.

One felt that within his cranium there was a well-oiled machine, with every bearing beautifully tuned, a complex apparatus that could be switched from first to top gear in a twinkling, and the answer to a problem produced with immediate and icy exactitude.

The "Old Man" was much warmer. He could be relied on to stand by any of his gunners who got into an acceptable kind of trouble, that is, a fist fight with a soldier from any neighbouring regiment. Off-duty, he appreciated a risqué joke and could tell one, too. When troubled or puzzled he'd screw in his monocle. This might, if he was really ruffled, be accompanied by an adjustment of his light sand-coloured tie. When amused he'd break into a surprisingly loud guffaw.

Despite their different personalities, the Old Man and the major were a good team, and if it came down to it, one could be as ruthless as the other. They didn't perhaps like one another very much. For one thing, the major didn't have much time for horses. I was invited to his room on select occasions for a private drink — always a good Scotch handed to me with due ceremony. He read poetry and had a few books on his mantelpiece, including a volume in classical Greek.

The colonel made no claim to being an intellectual. In his room he kept photographs of polo ponies and old regimental groups where the serried ranks of officers wearing riding breeches, tropical uniform and sun helmets were all, with one exception, very military and solemn. The exception he treasured. There on the top rank on the extreme right of the line of unsmiling, military, pith-helmeted figures at rigid attention, was a man standing out as obviously as a sore thumb. Sideways to the rest, arms folded in the exaggerated pose so favoured by soldiers of the Queen Empress, stood an officer. He was staring away from his comrades into the distant vistas of Empire, a huge false walrus moustache adorning his upper lip, and on his head a pillbox uniform cap from the century before.

"Poona, 1912," chuckled the Old Man. "Billy Blake, I'll never forget it. Visiting general and all that. All officers paraded for this picture. Billy sneaked that moustache and cap up to the dais, stood there on the edge of the line, whipped that ghastly moustache on and switched hats just as the wretch of a photographer put his head under his cape and pressed the button. Billy was a subaltern then. The general wanted him court-martialled and the commandant damn nearly shot him out of hand. Terrible row," he recalled with reminiscent glee.

"What happened to him, sir?"

"Oh, 1914, you know. Mons. Bad show. Lots of good fellows went with old Blake that day."

Bill Brewer, our captain and quartermaster (an officer if not quite a gentleman) was another member of our group. This man of sterling quality had just been promoted to the commissioned ranks. He had begun his service career as a boy soldier, slowly gaining in rank from bombardier (or gunner corporal) to sergeant and then to warrant officer. Whatever his "social acceptability," the colonel respected the quartermaster and always showed it. At forty-three he had reached the pinnacle of accomplishment for a man of his background. Despite this officer's commission he was generally regarded as a "ranker," a man rather on his own, as far as his fellow officers were concerned. He would retire from the army as a captain. He might, if he survived, even become a major. Few men of his social background achieved high rank.

The others included the motor transport officer, the adjutant (whose well-bred polish and studied nonchalance concealed the sharp wits and instincts of a buccaneer) and the administration and "attached" people like myself. I was by far the youngest of the lot. The battery messes were scattered and away from us, and they were much more light-hearted enclaves, for here youth prevailed and high jinks and spirits were to be expected.

The ranks of the enlisted men ("other ranks," as they were unceremoniously classified) consisted mostly, at least in the beginning, of long-term regulars. Many of them had been recalled to the colours after serving their time. They were mostly Londoners, or from the home counties around the capital, and they took their recalls philosophically, even cheerfully. They were used to the army and soon fell into their old ways. In many respects, I suppose they were like their forebears — Wellington's regulars of the Peninsular Wars, ill-educated, highly disciplined, earthy, ramrod straight, tough. Their officers seemed to belong to a different world.

The warrant and noncommissioned officers lacked the suave steeliness of their superiors, but they were every bit as hard. It was they who really handled the day-to-day discipline of the regiment. They had assimilated a number of territorial or militia NCOs who very quickly adopted the attitudes and outlook of their regular comrades. They had tremendous *esprit de corps*.

There were some splendid people among them, generous, warm-hearted and loyal friends. It was an honour for officers to be invited to the sergeants' mess on special occasions. There was an unwritten code of formality observed on both sides, at least in the early stages of such evenings, but as the beer and anecdotes began to flow, the sense of rank wore off, and for a few hours good fellowship prevailed.

Sometimes the impressions left could last for a lifetime. One night they broke into the hauntingly beautiful melody of the Eton "Boating Song." But the words were different. They sang the song of the mountain gunners of the Indian frontier.

> Smokin' my pipe on the mountings, sniffin' the mornin' cool,
> I walks in my old brown gaiters along o' my old brown mule,
> With seventy gunners be'ind me, an' never a beggar forgets
> It's only the pick of the Army that handles the dear little pets...

I looked through the tobacco smoke at the men around me. Many of them knew whereof they sang.

Like Kipling's poetry, they were a part of a vanishing era.

Chapter Eleven

It took me months to understand the subtleties and rigidities of the English class system. Social acceptability in the army seemed to revolve around a person's accent and former school.

Broad regional accents presented no great problem to me, but the different accents of middle- and upper-class Englishmen were quite perplexing, at least at first. The officer who had been to a mere grammar school (however old or distinguished) was not quite on the same social plane as the "public school" man.

Officers of this lower class kept appearing as the army expanded. The newcomers wore the same uniforms as the genuine articles, affected the same mannerisms, the same clipped moustaches and the same military ways, but to the initiated they kept giving themselves away by such subtleties as not holding their sherry glasses in quite the proper way. Thus they were exposed for what they were — impostors — "grammar school boys and the like," as one senior officer snorted disdainfully.

The strange thing was that the educated (or half-educated) Scot or Irishman would be accepted with great friendliness whatever his social background. I suppose our accents were as puzzling to them as theirs were to us.

And I suppose the educational systems of our quite different countries had something to do with it. The English public schools are, broadly speaking, boarding schools for sons of the well-to-do. Conformity in dress, manners, accent and outlook characterized the public school men who largely officered the prewar army. And the army, within itself, was caste conscious. The Guards stood alone. The cavalry were close behind, with the horse gunners (at least in the opinion of my friends) somewhere in between, while the great mass of fighting units followed in the wake of this elite in descending orders of social acceptance.

The kilted regiments were generally well regarded, as were certain fashionable London rifle regiments, but some units were hardly mentioned in polite conversation, it having been rumoured that some of their officers might not have attended the right schools.

Not that class distinction is confined to England. It was simply more blatant there, more pervasive. It flourished in Scotland in a bourgeois kind of way. It exists in North America in a more disguised fashion, and no doubt it thrives in tribal Africa. It is different, that is all.

Inherited money and titles seemed to mean more in England than in Scotland, where ambitious parents could talk about their offspring "getting on in life" without feeling they'd made a social *faux pas*.

Scotland has a few public schools patterned after the English model, but most Scots children attend local schools and, if destined for higher education, go on to one or other of the Scottish universities.

However, having acquired their degrees, many of them act on the remark of Dr. Samuel Johnson who wrote (rather huffily, I think), "The noblest prospect that a Scotchman ever sees, is the high road that leads him to London."

And once there, the educated Scot is received with a generosity and warmth that is not always conferred by upper-class Englishmen on their fellow countryman with the wrong accent.

I called in at the adjutant's office one morning on a matter of business. The adjutant had phoned me the previous afternoon.

"There's a fellow in the outer office," he'd said, "and I can't make him out at all. He seems a most reasonable chap, but I'm convinced after spending half an hour of my time on him that he's daft, or I am. So perhaps, Doc, old boy, you could see him and tell me which of the two of us should be in the loony bin. Funny thing," he added musingly, "all he says makes a queer kind of sense."

I saw the gunner, who for an hour made vague, seemingly sensible statements to me about his family affairs, until suddenly he confided in me that if I would only recommend him for a weekend's leave, he could go home and chop his wife into little pieces with an axe.

It seemed only appropriate that I should inform the adjutant that his initial impression had not been too far out, and that suitable action had been taken. The adjutant, urbane as ever, was glad to hear that his confidant was already being escorted towards the nearest military hospital.

That matter disposed of, he became confiding, closed the door to the outer office and bade me be seated. He came straight to the point. Mentioning the name of one of the officers in the headquarters mess where we both lived, he said, "We shall have to get rid of him, Doc, you know."

I had always thought that this particular officer was, if a little "different" in his ways, a competent chap at his job, and I said so.

"Oh well, he may be," replied my friend, "but he simply won't do, will he?"

"Why won't he?"

"I should have thought, Doc," said the adjutant, "that that is perfectly obvious. He isn't one of us."

"One of us?" I repeated questioningly.

"Yes, one of us. He's neither public school, Sandhurst nor Shop," explained the adjutant with courteous impatience.

"But, Dick," I protested innocently, "you fellows treat me like a long-lost brother, and I'm neither public school, Sandhurst nor Shop — and what's more, I don't give a damn either."

"My dear old fellow," replied the adjutant, "but don't you see — it really doesn't matter about you!"

"No?"

"No, of course not. You're not a regimental officer. He is. You're the regimental doctor, the sawbones — on loan from the good old Royal Army Medical Corps. It's all quite different. This fellow is a regular, a regimental officer, and he simply won't do. And after all, old boy," he concluded, almost affectionately, "if the truth be known—you're simply another bloody foreigner in for the duration."

Chapter Twelve

It was London, 1940, and wintertime. The city had endured a dreadful air raid during the night.

In the morning, as I made my way to the train to Scotland, smoke and the acrid smell of burning still hung in the air. Ambulances clanged their way through the streets and lines of hose writhed on the ground like great grey snakes as firemen struggled to douse the flames of the night before. Where buildings had collapsed, air raid workers swarmed over the rubble feverishly searching for survivors.

The attempt to bomb Britain to its knees was at its height and London was the primary target.

Rain was drenching down, yet hardly distrubing the drifting smoke. I was soaked to the skin as, lugging my steel helmet, gas mask and haver-sack, I passed the ticket collector and made for the northbound train.

Most of them still ran — amazingly, more or less on time — but it was announced that the express for Glasgow was going to be late in leaving.

Still, the guard was standing by his van, watch in hand and flag at the ready as I strode towards the luxury of a first-class compartment which was my due, as became an officer, and according to the ticket-of-leave in my pocket.

But the first-class compartments were crammed and my enquiries as to vacant seats were met with stony silence or apologetic smiles.

My search became feverish. The train was packed with troops. Anything would do, I thought, as I strode up and down the platform. Men were standing cheek-by-jowl in the corridors, and I had almost given up hope of boarding when a soldier leaned out of a window.

"Over here, bud. We'll get you in!"

And get me in they did. By dint of pulling from inside and a friendly push from outside by a passing porter, the deed was done.

I was no sooner standing in the corridor than there was a blast from the whistle and a series of giant puffs from the engine as we began to glide out of London and steam towards Scotland and a week's leave. It was then I noted that the fellows who had taken pity on me were kilted Highlanders. On their shoulders was the insignia, CANADA.

They suddenly realized that the battle-dress-clad figure beside them was an officer, and they fell silent. Soldiers seldom care to be in close proximity to strange officers, and they eyed me warily.

The one thing we shared, I thought as we stood there, was our drenching. The smell of warm wet wool became overwhelming as the train rolled northward. But as the steam began to rise from our clothes, so did the subdued geniality of my travelling companions. I was proffered a cigarette and took pains to assure them that my rejection of this kindness was due to my being a nonsmoker.

The lush, peaceful countryside of rural England passed before our eyes, villages whose ancient church towers dominated tree-lined streets as they have done for centuries. Rolling meadows that gave way to industrial cities of the Midlands, grim, red-brick places with houses crammed together in ugly rows, the railway tracks running parallel to dingy back yards where the household washing hung on clotheslines, forlornly trying to dry.

Beside the railway tracks in places were newly organized allotments where on vacant ground people grew vegetables to supplement their wartime diet. Dig for Victory, proclaimed the notices.

It was all new to my companions who exclaimed about this or that, then stood silent, breathing into one another's faces, swaying to and fro with the motion of the train. I felt sympathy with anyone who might have urgent need of a lavatory. That, in this crush, I feared, would be an unattainable goal.

I thought my travelling companions might be regretting their kindness in finding me a place, for my presence seemed to inhibit their conversation and they kept eyeing my insignia of rank. Suddenly, however, one of them reached into his haversack, produced a flask, took a swig from it and handed it to his mate. He in turn handed it to the third man who then silently offered it to me.

The ice was broken. Very soon my fellow travellers were telling me about this, their first visit to Scotland.

They were going to Glasgow. One of them was, of course, a MacDonald. With the Canadians there was always a MacDonald. He was going to see his never-seen-before Aunt Bessie. One Highlander who bore the name of Yahulnitsky was on his way to see his Aunt Jeannie. Perhaps his mother was also a MacDonald, but to have asked about his antecedents would have been both impolite and impolitic, for by now, with the help of a strange fluid known to them as rye and to me not at all, the journey was passing with increasing ease and speed.

My companions were rough diamonds. Their murderous use of the language would have been an offence against Fowler's *Modern English Usage*, but their admiration for Britain and its lonely stand against Nazism was unalloyed.

They asked me about Scotland and I tried to tell them something of its history, its dark and turbulent past as well as its present-day distinction in science and medicine. They weren't very interested in Lord Kelvin's experiments leading to the discovery of the atom, but when I told them about the feuds that for centuries had raged between the clans they became a rapt audience.

I told them of the long martial history of my homeland, of how for centuries the Scots had been renowned mercenaries. They were the Royal Guards of the kings of France. They were the Green Brigade of Gustavus Adolphus when that king of Sweden invaded Russia. And as we crossed the Scottish border, I recalled the Border Reivers, freebooting Scots horsemen who for generations ravaged the north of England. Honesty made me admit, albeit reluctantly, that their English cousins had always repaid their attentions with interest.

As the train climbed through the bare lowland hills, I talked of my own forebears, the Covenanters.

They had never heard of these puritanical Protestants of the sixteenth and seventeenth centuries who believed that both the Anglican and Roman churches were creations of the Devil and that they alone lived in grace. They were savagely hounded because of their stubborn beliefs. Their freedom was stripped from them, and in the end thousands of them, Highlanders and Lowlanders alike, signed the Scottish Covenant and took up arms to defend their rights.

The story that they went into battle carrying banners bearing the strange device "All for Christ. No Quarter Given" may be apocryphal, but I told my companions how, with the Covenant's ends achieved, the Protestant clergy in their own way became as tyrannical as their predecessors, grabbing for themselves the right to summon dissenters and defaulters to church and subject them in public to harsh rebuke.

But eventually it was my turn to ask questions. Why, I asked, had

Canadians in their thousands, and volunteers to a man, come to fight for a country of which they knew little?

My questions were met with blank looks. This, they told me, was the Old Country, and it was in trouble. That was all that was necessary, they seemed to say. Britain to them was as much a concept as it was a nation. Their grandparents had lived here. Their fathers had fought in Flanders in the Great War and one had died there. To them Great Britain meant tradition, law and order, decency. They were proud of their Scottish inheritance and their regiment, and I fell silent, remembering the words of "The Canadian Boat Song":

> From the lone sheiling of the misty island
> Mountains divide us, and the waste of seas—
> Yet still the blood is strong, the heart is Highland,
> And we in dreams behold the Hebrides.

But soon, though hours late, Glasgow, grimy as ever, crept into view. I guided them to the station entrance and the waiting tramcars and saw them on their way. As I took cordial leave of my Canadian kinsmen there were handshakes all round, and suddenly, unexpectedly and immaculately, salutes to the King's commission.

An hour later I walked up Kirk Road in my home town, just as I had done so often as a student, and there, standing at the sitting room window, waving to me, was my mother. I waved back, opened the garden gate and loped up the driveway.

It was a Thursday evening. For years on Thursdays my father and three of his friends, one of them the Reverend Mr. Alexander, had played bridge. Mother was just about to serve tea when I arrived, but courteously the players laid their cards on the table.

"Oh, son!" exclaimed my mother. "You're terribly late. What kept you?"

What kept me? What, indeed!

London was a world away from this quiet place, I thought. In a year I had graduated in more than medicine, but there was little point in expressing my thoughts, as fondly I put my arm round my mother's shoulder.

"Mother, dear," I said, smiling, "I'm late because the bloody train was late."

In an instant all was quiet. I had never before been known to swear.

Mr. Alexander turned to me. "My boy," he said, more in sorrow than in anger, "if your Covenanting forefathers could hear you use that word, they would turn in their graves."

Embarrassed, I was about to apologize when my father perched his spectacles on his forehead. It was a little habit he had.

"Alexander," he said, "D'ye really know much about the Covenanters?"

"James," said the minister, suddenly cautious, "I daresay I don't know as much as you do, but I'm told the martyrs died..."

"Ay, I know," said father. "They were shot, Bible in hand and with joy in their hearts. But the Covenanters weren't all like that, let me tell you. They were a hard-fighting, hard-riding, hard-swearing lot. But they fought for what they knew was right — civil and religious liberty. And if that's why my boy's in uniform, he's free to swear in this house as he pleases."

"Father," I said, "about the Covenanters — I think I've just travelled up from London with three of them!"

Chapter Thirteen

Capt. Ronald Flush and I shared rooms. We were "attached" officers — that is to say, officers of other corps seconded to the regiment. I was the regimental doctor, while Flush was the provost marshal, commander of a company of military policemen. While I revelled in mess life, the provost marshal held it in complete contempt, and while I was involved in all kinds of regimental activities, he was seldom seen. Even to his fellow officers he was a shadowy and, to some, a sinister figure. I found him an amusing chap, if only because he was one of the hardest boiled eggs I have ever encountered.

His relations with his fellow officers were not cordial, and so formality was observed on both sides. There was no light-hearted ribbing of Captain Flush, let me tell you. He was a very hard worker, frequently coming to his sleeping quarters in the early hours of the morning. I might turn in my cot as his Sam Browne belt jingled against the bedside chair, but usually he was as quiet as a mouse. In the mornings when I wakened, he'd be gone.

Flush had served all over the world. He was made for his job. He seemed to have no personal loyalties; only a loyalty to the service. I sometimes thought he was incapable of deep feeling, or had long ago chained his emotions. He was a pragmatic, stern philosopher and a martinet. The colonel didn't like him, and the Old Man had a soft spot for any of his gunners who got into trouble with Flush's "red caps." I suspect that Flush was pretty rigid when it came to being asked for any leniency.

His policemen were the same breed as himself, and as isolated. I used to feel sorry for them and their commander; but they didn't need my sympathy. Certainly Flush didn't. He was completely self-sufficient and as long as breakfast was on the table early enough, he made no complaints.

His leathery face made it difficult to judge his age, and he didn't confide in me. But I guessed that he was in his late forties. His travels had made him a very knowledgeable fellow on all kinds of subjects and when, on rare occasions, he chose to be amusing, he could, in his poker-faced way, be very amusing, indeed.

One of my fellow officers greeted me one morning.

"Did I hear Flush and you laughing last night?"

"Yes. Remind me to tell you some time — it was very funny."

"You mean he sometimes laughs?"

"Sure!"

"How extraordinary!"

That was Flush. He was tall and as lean as a ferret, and with his sharp face, long nose and cold eyes, he didn't look unlike one. He was responsible for military security, as well as the maintenance of good order and discipline — a broad field of endeavour, indeed, and in the latter case one of his areas of responsibility bordered on my own.

While I was responsible for the prevention and treatment of venereal disease, at least in the initial stages, the provost marshal was responsible for tracking down its sources. It was in this connection, following a lecture I gave him on the treatment of gonorrhoea with the new drug sulphonamide, that I found he was an expert in his own right. He had listened attentively to me, then he gave me a lecture on the social aspects of venereal disease in the military. The language he used was rough and ready, but the content of his remarks was a revelation to me.

He was an expert on the subject of sexual behaviour, and had a special interest in homosexuality. In many ways he was a man ahead of his time. He was neither moralistic nor judgemental. He was a clinical observer of people.

Venereal disease, he said, always had existed. So had homosexuality, and in some cultures was not frowned upon. It was simply a fact that soldiers infected with venereal disease were a financial liability and they reduced military efficiency. Furthermore, treatment of VD cost money. Homosexual soldiers were a double liability, he said, because they could cause emotional problems as well as spread disease. Military efficiency was his primary, and I sometimes thought his only, interest.

On one occasion the provost marshal "caught out" an officer, an individual he knew quite well. Despite the man's desperate pleading for some alternate way out, Flush took disciplinary action without a qualm. The officer was dismissed from the service. This action was typical of the man.

He said my education was incomplete — I knew nothing of the social or moral aspect of sexual behaviour. He was right. In the Calvinistic Scotland of my student days, psychiatry, with its probing into the dark and hidden turbulence of our minds, was held in about as much respect as the Roman liturgy. Sex, while known to exist, seemed to be much too raw a subject for the delicate ears of medical students. Today, of course, medical students do receive tuition in this very important area.

The provost marshal set out to remedy the defect in my training. A military doctor, he said, owed it to himself and his men to know more than the clinical basics of disease. His tuition was hard-nosed, and so I was shown the seamy side of life. I have always been grateful to him for the experience, because I gained a broader insight into human nature than I might otherwise have done. And I learned that a policeman must sometimes look at humanity from a different viewpoint than would a physician.

With the effective use of antibiotics, the disease problems of his day have largely gone. Trained soldiers were valuable men. One prostitute could infect a hundred men before the source of the disease was tracked down. That was one of Flush's responsibilities. He worked on the wise adage that prevention is better than cure.

One day he stalked into my office, ushered in by a rigidly erect medical orderly. His hard face told me he was looking for trouble. He favoured me with a salute, stared down his long nose at me and barked: "Have you been treating any officers on the quiet for VD?"

"No, of course not," I replied. "I didn't realize officers could even get VD."

There are occasions when even a trace of levity can be injudicious, and this was one of them.

"Don't try me on, Doctor. If you say you haven't treated any officers with clap, then of course that's the end of it. You know the rules as well as I do. But they're getting it all the same — from somewhere, by God."

"How do you manage to get to know this kind of thing?" I asked. "Nothing goes on in this area but you unearth it like a dog after a bone!"

"It's my job, Doc, and there's nothing smart about it. It's part of my duty: security. How do I know? Because there's a draft of officers — very hush-hush — assembled to leave. They have their own M.O. who gives them inoculations for the tropics. Three of them came down with VD this week and it was reported to me. Their doctor thinks there may be more cases."

He paused thoughtfully, quietly tapping on the top of my desk with his cane. "They got it somewhere, didn't they? Unless, of course, you believe in the lavatory seat theory." A sour smile flickered momentarily across his face. "Some of the victims appear to do so," he concluded.

"Well, I'm sorry, Flush. I can't help you. There are no officers in this outfit affected."

Always the exacting clinician, he corrected me: "That you know of!"

The tapping of his cane was the only sound to be heard. Suddenly he said, "Tell you what. I believe I know the source of the problem — the Turret Club. It's open to officers. There are some high-class prostitutes in town — cleared out of London to avoid the Blitz. A lot of officers frequent that place, and so do these women. Now it's your duty, isn't it, to take preventive measures against the spread of VD?"

"Yes, of course, but I don't know what you're getting at."

"I could do with your help, that's what I'm getting at. If I go there alone, somebody'll spot me, and all we'll do is move 'em on. But you, young fellow me lad, if you and I went there together, in plain clothes for dinner — that'd be different, wouldn't it now?"

He nodded at me, hitched down his tunic at the back, adjusted his Sam Browne belt at the front, stroked his finely waxed moustache and looked at me expectantly.

"What about it, Doc? I want to know what goes on in there. Anyway, it'd be an experiment."

"Oh!" I replied hesitantly, "it's not my kind of thing. I don't know."

"If it *was* your kind of thing, I wouldn't be asking you. I'm not suggesting you get into bed with one of them to prove my point. All you've got to do is come with me. Look," he finished, "if it'll help you to make up that north British mind of yours, I'll pay for the meal. How about it?"

It was done. I had accompanied my roommate once or twice before on his little forays. What he was up to was sometimes beyond me, and the gallant captain didn't always enlighten me, but somewhere in the shadows, or in a distant corner of a hotel lounge, I knew there were one or two of his men, also in civilian clothes, quietly watchful.

So I booked for dinner. We arrived together, relaxed in our civilian suits. My friend selected the table and succeeded in becoming inconspicuous so quickly that I admired his expertise anew.

The food was good. I enjoyed the meal. My companion was quietly jocular and knew his wines. We were seated in a spot where we could look around, though with the subdued lighting it was somewhat difficult to see every corner of the dining room. It must at one time have been a large hall, for surrounding it on the upper floor was a balcony. Made of highly polished dark wood, the stairway to the second floor was, like the rest of the place, sumptuously carpeted in a dark red colour, while the rooms leading off from the balcony above us could hardly be seen for curtains of the same colour, tastefully draped along the dark oak of the balustrades.

Elegantly furnished, the linen spotless, with the pianist playing the kind of music that would have appealed to my maiden aunt, the atmosphere of the place was innocence itself. Expensive, perhaps, but innocent. I said so.

"It's a high-class whorehouse," was the grunted response.

There were no officers in sight, and not a single female, but the P.M. had been taking a quiet interest in a civilian seated at a table. He gently indicated that I should watch the man.

"He's a homosexual," he said softly. "It's none of my business — yet. But if he's not waiting to be picked up, I'm a Dutchman." Shortly a second man appeared and joined the first. Drinks were brought and the two men appeared to be deep in conversation.

"It's a perfectly innocent looking situation to me," I whispered. "These two chaps could be here for dinner or anything."

Flush just stared me down and grunted, " 'Or anything' is right."

Before very long the men rose and strolled up the elegant stairway to the balcony. They could have been on their way to a meeting, and, puzzled, I asked my colleague how his suspicions arose.

"Experience, I suppose. Nothing I could swear to in a court of law. There's a way of accosting somebody. You learn by observing. I just suspect, that's all, and I don't give a damn either," said my companion, leaning over and refilling my glass, "for these two aren't my responsibility. They're civilians. Still," he went on, "we can't stay here all night, Doc. If something doesn't happen soon, by God, you'll have to pay for the return meal. And that, old boy, would hurt, wouldn't it?"

But just then the door opened and a group of young officers entered the now busy dining room and made their way to reserved tables. Soon they were joined by others, and the place began to take on quite a military flavour. The wine began to flow, dinner was served, and soon a lively party was in progress.

It was at this point that a really shapely creature joined the group. It would be incorrect to say that I took no notice of her. She was what was known in my student days as "a smasher." Soon she was joined by another eye-catching blonde with a very fetching figure, and ere long other luscious creatures had made their appearance. Arms were thrown affectionately round khaki-clad necks, and khaki-clad arms discreetly encircled shapely waists.

"There y' go," commented my companion in a significant tone.

I must admit I was a trifle miffed. "How come," I asked with some annoyance, "that none of these stunners took notice of me — if you're right?"

"Virtue, dear boy, and innocence are written on your face for all to see," replied my host, with a hard grin. "Besides, I suspect that little party was laid on, so to speak."

The party was becoming hilarious, with all the verve and dash of gallant young men and the grace and laughter of beautiful women. I watched, entranced yet wistful, an observer, aloof yet yearning. Flush was stuffing a dry roll into his mouth and draining his wine, paying the group nonchalant attention.

Several couples drifted upstairs, to be followed by others. My companion ordered a couple of brandies. They were brought to our table. He then requested the bill. He had been toying with his brandy, sipping it. Now he looked at his watch, swallowed the remaining contents of his glass and said quietly, "Outside."

As we made our inauspicious way to the exit, two groups of somewhat bulky gentlemen, it seemed, had also finished their meals and had risen to their feet. The captain and I went home to the cubbyhole we shared. The P.M. switched off the light. "You should be satisfied, Doc. Now you don't have to pay for that return meal, do you?" And with a sardonic laugh, he turned over and went to sleep like a child.

In the morning when I woke, he was gone. I passed the Turret Club on my way to morning sick parade. The iron gate was padlocked and a large notice bore the word Closed.

Captain Flush, as I said before, was an early riser.

Chapter Fourteen

It was June 1941.

"Doc, what's this about the Tank Corps?"

"The Armoured Corps, Dick."

Dick West looked up from his desk. I had called into the adjutant's office with a report he wanted, and his question had caught me unawares. He was reading a document which obviously referred to me.

"Armoured Corps, then. A rose," sniffed the adjutant, "smells as sweet by any other name."

I had spent a happy year with the regiment, but it was time to move.

"Do you know anything about the Tanks?" he asked.

"No, but I've read Fuller, and Liddell Hart."

"You've read? How very helpful that must have been," rejoined my friend, whose literary interests were confined to the *Sporting Times* and the *Illustrated London News*. "Well, then, you don't know anything about the Tank Corps, do you, but you've read! Tell me, do you know any of their officers?"

"No."

"There you are, you see. You don't know a damned thing, do you? Well, I do, and let me tell you, the Tank Corps is the bitter end."

Gathering his thoughts for a further assault, he looked out of the window before turning his attention to me.

"The officers," he went on, "just let's take the officers. They're not so much officers as devotees: glorified bloody mechanics grovelling in the mud under those dreadful, filthy, oily, smelly machines of theirs. Appalling! Simply appalling! And that's where you're going? You'll regret it, let me tell you."

He shook his head, more in sorrow than in anger, which I knew was usually contrived anyway.

"They're just not like us, Doc, that's all that can be said about it."

"Dick," I said, seriously enough, "you fellows would like to deliver your goods at the speed of Caesar's legions. Coal merchants in Scotland deliver their goods at thirty miles per hour. So do the tanks. Speed will win this war, old boy," I said, "at thirty miles per hour."

He glared at me, momentarily taken aback. His recovery, as usual, was swift. "Only occasionally, Doc. Only occasionally. You'd be surprised. Tracks break, don't y' know, and drop off. Engines fail — that kind of thing!"

"Well Dick, the die is cast."

Dick had cooled off. "I realize that, Doc, and we wish you well, but all the same...the Tanks!" The point was worrying him.

"They really are different, their officers," he mused. "They don't seem to play golf, for instance, and they don't ride at all, as far as I can see. And you know," he added, a sudden thought having struck him, "I don't believe I know one of them that belongs to a decent London club." It was the final, the saddest, the most profound verdict he could bring himself to deliver.

My posting would come in due course, and I continued with my duties. I had not been a military figure, though I had acquired some new skills, few of them medical. I had, admittedly, trudged along behind a column of men the odd time, more for the fun of it than in the line of duty. I had never attended a formal parade and didn't expect to, until one morning on leaving the mess with my friend, Captain Brewer, he tapped the notice board with his swagger stick and read that the regiment would parade that afternoon at 1400 hours.

"All officers will attend," he intoned, touching the notice with his cane for emphasis. Transferring the end of his swagger stick from the notice board to my abdomen, which he prodded for effect, he added, "And that means you, Doc, for once. Part Two Orders, see?"

"Parade? Me?"

"Yes, that's right — you. You're an attached officer, so you stand in on the left of the line of officers. Get it? Be there."

It was 1400 hours — to be precise, a minute or so after — when I made my appearance. The regiment was drawn up, battery by battery, hundreds of men, all gleaming and glistening and sweating as I stepped into place. The headquarters officers were not placed in any prominent position, and I was grateful for that.

The colonel, resplendent in service dress, decorations flashing in the afternoon light, riding boots shining like twin suns, strolled up and down the line, exchanging a word here and there, occasionally thwacking one of his boots with the riding crop he carried. We were awaiting the arrival of a very senior military dignitary.

His stroll brought him level with me, and after glancing at me in obvious surprise, out came the monocle as he inspected me further.

"I say, Doc old boy, how nice of you to come!"

"That's quite all right, sir. It's a pleasure."

He turned and sauntered off, but soon he was back, and again, as he drew level with me, he stopped.

"Doc, what made you turn out for this parade?"

"Part Two Orders, sir. 'All officers will attend,' " I repeated.

I didn't realize you paid such attention to Part Two Orders," he murmured musingly, seemingly puzzled.

"Well, sir, actually," I told him, "Q told me to be here, sir. He brought the notice to my attention."

"Did he, indeed! So Q told you?"

The monocle was in place and surveyed the line of officers standing at ease. The quartermaster was beginning to look a bit comfortable in front and his tunic was just a little in advance of the rest of the line of officers. He was three or four down from me and I could see that protrusion of his out of the corner of my eye.

The monocle zeroed in on Bill like a laser.

"Well, Doc," said the colonel, "it's really terribly good of you to come. But I realize you're awfully busy, and really, old boy, you needn't stay, you know. As a matter of fact," he added, lowering his voice to a tone of confidentiality, "I do believe you're spoiling the look of my entire regiment," and with that sudden guffaw of his, he strolled away.

So did I.

A few weeks later I strolled into a very different setting. The long, practised, seemingly leisurely professionalism of the gunners was far behind me. So was my pampered life as the regimental doctor.

I had expected to go overseas at short notice, and Janet and I had married in 1941, but instead of going abroad I was sent to one of Britain's newly formed armoured divisions.

There, thirty young men, medical corpsmen and transport drivers, looked upon me as their leader. Already trained soldiers, they were a well-knit unit, but the practicalities of armoured warfare were as new to them as they were to me. Together we had to learn the use of compasses and map reading and master the art of keeping trucks and ambulances not just on roads made slippery by mud from the preceding tanks, but in the right place in the right convoy — not always the easiest of tasks to accomplish.

And then, as the colonel had so jocularly noted at that last regimental parade, my knowledge of foot drill was, to say the least, sketchy. There was nothing jocular about it now. I had to learn — fast.

Commanders varied in their approach to training. Some were more leisurely than others, but when I and my little company moved from the lush Downs of southern England to a division training on the moors of Yorkshire, we realized we were in the hands of a master.

The commanding general, whose courteous front concealed a will of steel, demanded perfection. He seemed to be everywhere. The mere glint of a watery sun on the improperly camouflaged windshield of a single truck could call down on some astounded driver the wrath of the divisional commander himself, passing by chance in an armoured car.

But nothing could distract from the beauty of the Yorkshire moors with their towns nestling in the dales — not even the forced marches or sleep snatched behind some drystone wall at the edge of a field. I have to admit, however, that after the war I found I had lost any romantic enthusiasm for organized hiking parties or sleeping under the stars.

The average age of the young men in my section was nineteen or twenty; the sergeant (known behind his back as Dad) was twenty-eight and I, in my middle twenties, was next in line for the old age pension. Their youth, however, was unaccompanied by any sense of false modesty. They let it be known that they were "the best," and certainly they accomplished their tasks with skill, resourcefulness and sometimes even panache.

One of their allotted duties could involve unpleasantness and risk. At the foot of the steep, pathless cliffs that abounded on the northeast coast, bodies were sometimes washed ashore, and our field ambulance had the task of recovering them.

The corpses were usually those of seamen or airmen, for our merchant navy convoys were frequently attacked by German bombers. Casualties on both sides were inevitable.

I was the duty officer one winter morning when the telephone rang and a police sergeant told me a body had been seen washing to and fro in the surf at the foot of a cliff some seven miles away. I summoned the duty ambulance crew, gave them their instructions, bade them take care, and to report to me as soon as the body had been brought up the cliff to the ambulance.

Privates Brimacomb, MacEvoy and Driver Sewell, assuring me that all would be handled with their usual efficiency and aplomb, took their departure.

Hours passed and I became anxious. I had just summoned the motorcycle dispatch rider to conduct a reconnaissance when the phone rang.

It was Private Bimacomb, RAMC.

"We've got him up, sir, and he's in the ambulance."

"Is he ours or theirs?"

"It's a German airman, sir."

"I expected you to report a couple of hours ago. Have you had trouble?"

"Only a bit, sir. We had to use ropes, but that wasn't the trouble, sir, although it took us a long time to get the body up, sir, and now the ambulance is in the ditch, sir. We'll need help to get it out."

"How did you get ditched?"

"Well, the tanks had come off the moors and a lot of wet mud fell off their tracks. The road's in very bad condition, sir."

"Right. I'll send a repair truck," and having obtained directions, I was about to put the phone down when Private Brimacomb spoke again.

"That's not all, sir!"

"What else is wrong?"

"Nothing, sir, except the body. It's been in the sea for a long time and it's badly decomposed. It's almost in two bits, sir."

"I am sorry, Brimacomb. I'll get help to you as soon as possible."

"Thank you, sir, I hope you will, sir." And then in one breath: "MacEvoy's sitting on one side of the ambulance with his foot braced against the corpse, sir, to stop it from sliding onto the floor, and it's an 'orrible sight, and it smells terrible, and you know, sir" — plaintively — "we've not had our lunch yet, sir!"

It's difficult today to realize that such a spritely lot have now become elderly gentlemen.

Chapter Fifteen

The end of the war was in sight and I was once again a "proper doctor," as someone said, in charge of a small army "hospital" in rural England.

I was strolling towards the office one morning when I met Corporal Stinton hurrying towards me.

"It's brigade headquarters on the phone, sir. For you. It's the brigade major."

"Oh!"

Brigade H.Q. was only occasionally on the phone and never for trifles. But the brigade major himself — that was different! And for me, too! Brigade majors were important people. They stood, so to speak, at the right hand of their gods — the brigadiers-general — and furthermore they were often the harbingers of bad news.

I smartened my step and reached for the telephone, held towards me by an orderly room clerk who seemed to think it had an infectious disease.

"Morning, Major," I said with feigned nonchalance.

"Good morning to you, Doctor," replied that cool voice at the other end. "The brigadier feels that you should be advised that your hospital is in the direct path of a forthcoming tour by the general, who has expressed his intention of inspecting your establishment. He intends to inspect most units under his command and feels that a medical unit should be included in the tour. Next Thursday at 1100 hours. He may stop for lunch."

He paused. "Have you anything to say?" he asked, having let his directive sink in.

My mind was racing. The brigadier-general was one thing. His infrequent visits were pleasant enough. He was a jovial chap, was the brigadier, a man in his early fifties, who would cheerfully accept a glass of sherry from a humble medical officer. But an inspection by the general-officer-commanding — that was a horse of another colour! I almost gulped.

"I'm shattered," I replied to the brigade major.

"That wasn't quite the answer I expected," replied that dignitary coldly. "Do you need any help? The brigadier has instructed me to offer you a work crew if you need the place tidied up — paint work, that kind of thing."

Still off balance a bit, I assured the distant voice that we were in good shape.

"Very well, if you say so," and the conversation was at an end.

Stories about the general abounded. He was held in great awe, even fear. That he should descend from such Olympian heights to inspect my humble establishment was enough to put me off my lunch. However, summoning my two NCOs, I directed that in the three days that were left to us, the place must be scrubbed, rescrubbed and then soaked in so much antiseptic that even the strongest germ would quail at the very thought of coming near.

I was in charge of a forty-bed medical unit designed for the treatment of relatively minor illnesses. Sick soldiers could be looked after for a week or two, and then, if no better, transferred to military hospitals. The brigade major's appellation of "your hospital" was flattering to say the least.

Still, I prided myself that the unit was efficient. Slackening of standards by medical orderlies was met by dark threats of being "posted back to the RAMC depot for a bit of smartening up." At the depot dwelt demonic creatures called drill sergeants, and I seldom had trouble.

The "hospital" was a requisitioned mansion. The grounds were well kept, thanks in large part to the volunteer work of convalescent patients. The war had not always been kind to them and they welcomed a few days of weeding and hoeing before returning to their regiments.

The days of ordering bed-ridden soldiers to "lie at attention" during the rounds of military medical officers had been consigned to the best place for them — the military historical rubbish heap. Our patients were treated like human beings, and only the few "old soldiers" — of whatever age — abused the routine. Those, I fancied, I could deal with.

Army medical officers were notoriously hard-hearted individuals, ever on the lookout for malingerers and scrimshankers, and I could put on as hard-faced an act as any of them. I was, I fancied, as capable as anyone of beating old soldiers at their little games. Almost, I felt, I was one myself.

In our hospital we prided ourselves especially on the quality of the food. Our corporal-cook was an old-time regular soldier. His long-service stripes reached halfway up his arm, and under his eagle eye the cooking was excellent. Despite my growing trepidation, I knew that if the general stayed for lunch, he would be well satisfied.

The one real problem was the state of the corporal's cooking utensils. They were well used. Where they weren't black, they were brown. Still, no one as ignorant as I should ever interfere with such an artist and until now I had allowed the matter to pass. But no longer. A crisis was at hand. My very fate could be in the balance.

I hastened to the kitchen, took the corporal aside, appealed to his sense of loyalty — in descending order of priority — to myself, the hospital, the Royal Army Medical Corps and his country, and finished by saying that if the pots weren't spotless inside two days, he would be cooking certain of his own appendages for my morning meal.

Corporal Matthews merely beamed at me. "Ah'r, don't you worry, zur," he said in his broad west-country accent. "You just come with me and I'll show you something as'll set even the general 'imself back on 'is heels."

Throwing open one of the kitchen cupboards, he cried, "There you are, zur. All ready for 'is nibs on Thorsday, zur."

Row upon row, flat against the wall, was the most immaculate display of cooking utensils I have ever seen. They shone like bright stars against the dark oak of the old cupboard. I stood agape.

Corporal Matthews's broad face broke into a grin.

"Aye, zur, that's wot comes of being an old soldier, zur. You see, zur, inspecting kitchens were always a great thing with hinspecting officers before the war. So I borrowed this set, zur — they'll never be missed," he added humorously, "and so I'm ready for the GOC. An' 'e isn't even goin' to see t'other pots, take it from me, zur, never you fear, zur."

Tottering slightly, I retired to the office, leaving the matter of the cooking utensils in the corporal's capable hands.

Came Thursday. At 1100 hours precisely the general's car swept up the driveway. He was alone, apart from his driver, a couple of military policemen on motorbikes, and an NCO, presumably a clerk.

His entourage was immediately whisked off to the care of Corporal Matthews, for we were not unaware of the value of public relations work. An excellent lunch awaited them.

I was at the front door of my hospital to meet the general as his car

75

drew up. A tallish, well set-up man, the general acknowledged my salute with a perfunctory wave of his cane, looked over the ivy clinging to the stone walls of the portico and announced that he would begin immediately by touring the wards. An early lunch had just been served, and the patients, encouraged by one of Corporal Matthews's more notable efforts, one after another expressed their satisfaction.

Stony-faced but, I thought, impressed by their enthusiasm, the general moved from one room to the next.

"And now," he barked, "the kitchens, Doctor."

This was it, I thought, as I led the way. But Corporal Matthews was ready. There he stood in immaculate white overalls with his helpers, similarly attired, standing at attention in the background. The place was spotless and I breathed a sigh of relief. My ordeal was almost over.

The general prowled about, looking into spotless pots that bubbled with deliciously smelling concoctions, then asked: "May I see the rest of your cooking utensils, Corporal?"

It was just the moment Corporal Matthews had been waiting for. Triumphantly he threw open the cupboard. There was the spare set all agleam and flashing in the diffuse sunlight. The general looked at them.

"Marvellous," he said. "Simply marvellous — but where are the ones you use every day? This is the spare set, I'd say? Eh, Corporal?"

Old Matthews's face was a picture, registering hurt, astonishment, injured innocence and — was it fear? — all in one fleeting expression.

My own feelings could hardly be described.

The general just stood there silently, waiting for an answer.

"I'll wager I know where they are too, Corporal. It would take me about five minutes to find them. I'd head for the nearest shrubbery and there they'll be hidden, in a state beyond description, I've no doubt. But I don't have five minutes. Come, Doctor, I must be on my way."

Shattered, I walked with him to his car. His retinue was standing waiting, and as soon as he appeared, they snapped to attention.

Silently he made to step into the car, then stopped, turned to me and, with an almost imperceptible nod in the directon of the kitchen, said: "He's an old soldier. Well, so am I. But it grieves me to think that a corporal-cook could even dream of pulling off that old trick on a general!"

Chapter Sixteen

A week or two went by. I was still in a somewhat delicate state of mental health following the general's inspection, but recovering with the help of Corporal Matthews's cooking, when there was another phone call.

This time it was from my medical colonel, an affable Irishman and a career officer of the Royal Army Medical Corps.

"Well, now," he said, "it's been decided that you need a change of air. So you're being transferred to general headquarters — for medical and administrative duties. Your relief is on his way."

"When do you want me to report, sir?"

"The day after tomorrow would do just fine. At eight o'clock in the morning, m'boy." And he rang off.

I had been working at headquarters for about a month when one evening I was ordered to report to the general's quarters, a requisitioned mansion a few miles away from the main buildings.

Apart from his living quarters, the house contained offices for the most senior of his staff. There was an atmosphere of frigid formality about the place and that impression was not lessened by the austere colonel who bade me follow him to the general's bedroom.

I was ushered in by the colonel who stood at attention as rigidly as any orderly-room sergeant, and I smartly followed suit.

The general may have been propped up in bed and looking none too well, but he was still the general and I stood there at attention. The colonel retired, closing the door behind him. The general looked at me.

"Sir," I said, breaking the silence and mouthing the obvious, "you wish to see me?"

"I require your professional advice, yes. I'm ill, with what I do not know. Kindly examine me and give me your opinion."

I had already noted the herpes on his lips, a classical sign of pneumonia. He was breathing rapidly, his face was flushed, and I guessed he had lobar pneumonia, a spot diagnosis that I confirmed when I carried out a full examination.

He took the news without comment for a moment, then asked, "Can you take care of me here?"

"You'd be safer in hospital, sir. Your pneumonia is quite severe."

"I do not wish to go to hospital. What treatment would they give me?"

"Sulphonamide, sir. It's very effective in the treatment of pneumonia."

Sulphonamide was the first of the drugs that could literally kill bacteria, the forerunner of penicillin, which would appear a year later.

"Can you treat me with sulphonamide?"

"Yessir."

"Then kindly do so."

I hesitated, then said, "Sir, if your pneumonia doesn't respond, I would have to insist on hospital treatment."

Coldly my commander inquired, "Insist? Doctor — *you* would have to insist?"

I stood there, sweating quietly, not knowing how to respond, but suddenly he said, "You're quite right, of course. Can you begin the treatment at once?"

So I gave him an initial dose of the drug, snapped to attention again, said goodnight and with great relief headed for the door.

I'd just reached it when he spoke again. "One moment, Doctor."

"Oh God," I thought. "What have I done wrong?"

The general looked at me steadily.

"Most officers are afraid of me. Why are you not afraid of me?"

I was completely taken aback, but there have been times in my life when instinctively I have known I was being tested in some way, and this I knew was such a time. His cold blue eyes appraised me as I searched for a suitable reply. Suddenly, the words slipped out before I could stop myself.

"Sir," I replied, "last night I saw a very sick soldier. He was lying in a cot in a Nissen hut in his shirt-tail between two army blankets. Tonight, sir, I see you in silk pyjamas, in this mansion. Two very ill men, who may share the same thought — that they are facing their Maker.

"Sir," I went on, "I've taken on a great deal of responsibility tonight. If I was afraid of you, I doubt if I'd be of much use to you."

Then I stood there, rigidly erect and sweating, cold though I was. He nodded. "Goodnight to you. You will call tomorrow." It was an order, not an invitation.

"A strange man," I thought, as I was driven back to headquarters in the staff car that had brought me, for what he had said was true. Many of his officers, even the very senior ones, stood in great awe of him. And yet his question had been put politely, almost analytically and without a trace of the arrogance I might have expected.

An X-ray confirmed the diagnosis, and for the next two weeks I waited anxiously for the drug to work. My medical colonel insisted that I take full charge of the case. I had the impression that the colonel didn't want to touch the general with a forty-foot bargepole, never mind a stethoscope! I felt my responsibilities deeply and once or twice I faltered and suggested that my patient might want to change his mind and go to hospital, but he refused to hear of it.

"I do believe, Doctor," he once said frostily, "that I have more confidence in you than you have in yourself," and that was the end of that. He was an uncomplaining patient, but none of my visits were what might be called relaxed.

In the end, the sulphonamide contained the infection and late one afternoon when I arrived for my daily visit, I found the general, in uniform, sitting at his desk. He had lost weight and his tunic hung on his once brawny frame, but there was no doubt that the GOC was in full circulation.

He rang a bell and his batman appeared, carrying a tray on which stood two glasses, a flask and a siphon of soda water.

"We're going to celebrate my recovery," said the general, "and your dismissal from the case. I do believe," he went on, "that I've been a more difficult patient than you would care to admit. But I will send for you from time to time, for I have always had a great interest in the profession of medicine."

There began a strange, formal, yet lasting friendship. From time to time and always in the evenings, I would receive summonses to the general's quarters. I was always offered a Scotch, told to make myself comfortable (a task that was, at least in the beginning, accomplished with some difficulty) and for an hour or two we would talk.

Gradually my awe of the man was replaced with growing respect, and later, with a kind of affection. He had a keen and well-informed mind and often surprised me with his observations. He particularly respected the British soldier, but said that with the coming of sophisticated weaponry the army would have to attract and train educated men, who would be well-paid professionals. For a man of his class and background, he was surprisingly liberal in his outlook, having much sympathy for working people who, he felt, deserved better education, social conditions and more of a chance to better themselves, and hence their country.

Much of his life had been spent in India. Like so many of his kind, he was drawn to the country, to the life there, and to Indians of his own class, for whom he had much respect. For the poor of India he had nothing but pity.

"Of course," he once said, "we'll be thrown out at the end of this war. A few hundred thousand troops can't control millions of resentful Indians, treated like second-class citizens in their own country. It could have been different if we'd been more enlightened, perhaps. We won't lose the Indian Empire because of brutality, Doctor. We're not a brutal people, as people go. No. We'll lose India because of snobbery."

I went home to Scotland on leave. Janet managed to get leave from her hospital and a neighbour decided that he was going to put on a little house party for us.

It was all very Scottish. While the ladies retired to my friend's drawing room where small glasses of sherry were handed out with much decorum, their spouses headed for the kitchen where an array of whisky bottles stood on the kitchen table. Ladies in Scotland were not supposed to drink whisky at all, and their husbands preferred to down the stuff in the company of other men before participating in social occasions. However, it was a memorably happy evening, and afterward my old friend and I sat alone by the fireside talking.

Suddenly he said, "This general of yours — what's his first name?"

"I'm hardly on first-name terms with the general," I smiled, "but I do know it." And I told him.

My friend, cupping his brandy glass in his hands, stretched out his legs towards the fire, stared into the flames for a minute or so, then said: "It must be the same chap. Is he as forbidding a character as he used to be?"

Astounded, I exclaimed, "Bob, don't tell me you know him!"

Bob, still staring into the fire, conjuring up long-forgotten memories, took his time about replying.

"Aye," he said, nodding his head. "If it's the same man, then I once knew him. Though I doubt if anybody knew him very well. He was my company commander in 1916. I was a second-lieutenant then. Second-lieutenants, you know, didn't live very long in 1916 — about three months if they were lucky. I was lucky.

"I got so badly shot up I was in hospital till the end of the war. He must have been nearly thirty and I was twenty-one. He was one of the few surviving regular officers in that outfit. The rest of us were volunteers, but we were civilian volunteers — Kitchener's army — 'temporary officers and gentlemen'! Your general was very distant to us, and at first I thought it was because in his eyes we weren't quite up to his image of what officers should be like. But I changed my mind eventually. He was a man on his own, and probably lonely in his own way.

"We had a very brave sergeant. He was a regular, an example of what a good NCO should be. He looked after his men, was a good disciplinarian, but I've seen him volunteer to go out on a dangerous job just to break in an inexperienced chap, show him the dangerous places.

"Well, one day in a nasty little action, that sergeant just turned and ran away. It wasn't even a big action. It was the kind of thing he must have handled dozens of times, and very well, too.

"You know what happened, of course. They court-martialled him for desertion in the face of the enemy. He was sentenced to be executed by firing squad. That man of all men!

"They did it, too. No excuses taken. They shot him with all due ceremony. But if ever a man fought for a fellow human being's life, it was your general. He was a major then. He stood by that sergeant as if he were his brother. He fought desperately to save him. I was told later — for I'd been shot up by then — that the sergeant asked the major if he'd attend the execution. And he did. He stood beside him almost to the bitter end.

"It took courage to do that, and it took courage to face up to all that military brass on the court martial the way he did. I used to think it couldn't have done his career as a regular soldier much good — but then, with your comrades being slaughtered beside you day in and day out, life and your values become very different. But what a man! And you wouldn't think there was an emotional inch in him, would you?"

My leave ended and I went back to duty.. I kept that story to myself, but one evening a few months later, out of the blue, the general started to talk about bravery — moral as well as physical.

"Every man," he said quietly, "has it in him to be both a coward and a hero. Nowadays," he went on, "we have doctors in the army who have the training and the authority to diagnose the danger signs of a man's breakdown. And they can do something about it, too — save useful lives by transferring men to other duties, even temporarily. The army wasn't always like that. They used to shoot men for being what they called cowards. Thank God we don't do that any more.

"You know," he said thoughtfully, "I'm convinced that diarrhoea—or constipation — could make a coward of a hero!"

Chapter Seventeen

It had been a tiring day. At one unit after another I had had to submit myself to interrogation from one commander after another. My questioners wanted to know what was going on at "the top." The general was being a holy terror and rumour had it that the new brigadier was "difficult." I was expected to clarify all the gossip.

The medical problems had been trying that day, too, and I was relieved when my driver turned off the main road and we trundled up the winding drive past the ornamental lily pond to the headquarters building. We drew up at the front entrance of the mansion that served as our H.Q. It was late afternoon.

Driver Oxley had been detailed to act as my chauffeur. As he opened the car door for me, he crashed his hobnailed boots into the crumbling cement of the portico, snapped rigidly to attention and favoured me with a superb salute. That salute was his sole military virtue. His vehicle was not properly maintained, and it had broken down that day.

Acknowledging his ceremonial with scant patience, I went to my colonel's office and dropped the day's reports into the in-tray. The place was empty. Even that infallibly correct individual, the sergeant-major, had departed. Feeling that a drink before dinner might improve my mood, I headed for the mess. There was a line-up at the bar. It was a workaday army by that time.

My fellow officers were lawyers, teachers, businessmen, and I noticed idly that they were all wearing battle dress. All but one. His back was towards me and I could see that he was a stranger. I noticed that his service dress was not made of wartime barathea but of cavalry twill, and my mind went back to 1940 to my first regiment, to the colonel and Dick West with their impeccable cavalry twill uniforms. "This fellow," I thought, "is a prewar soldier," and when he half turned, looked over his shoulder at me, those cool eyes appraising me, I was sure of it.

"Ah!" he said, eyeing my insignia, "the doctor." Turning his head from me, he called peremptorily, "Barman, bring the doctor a drink — Scotch, I should think," and continued his previous conversation as if I had never existed. It was only when he turned full onto me a few minutes later that I saw his campaign ribbons from World War One and the clerical collar. Somehow I hadn't expected that.

"And now, Doctor," he said, as he smiled and proffered his hand, "we're to be colleagues for a time. While you look after the physical needs of your people, I shall attend to things spiritual. Have another drink."

He was a good-looking fellow, in his middle forties, I judged. Slimly built and erect, he would have looked well on parade with his men, rather than preaching to them, and I said so to one of my acquaintances that night. My friend, a solicitor in civilian life, laughed.

"Well you might say that. He's an ex-regular. He left the army and entered the Church. He has a rather good living somewhere in the south. Quite 'county,' I believe."

Five years before, Dick West and company would have taken the "county" (or decidedly upper-class) connection for granted, but it was easy to see that the padre fitted smoothly into a mess. Part spiritual adviser, part social worker, he was still part soldier, and the men saw that in him.

Some time previously I had looked after a young soldier taken ill while on leave. It wasn't a serious illness, but the young man's mother was grateful to me. Her husband and she owned a sizable estate, which was becoming neglected, as he was overseas and the estate workers were in the forces. An elderly gamekeeper, more from loyalty than need, had come out of retirement and, with the help of an aging groom, kept the grounds in some kind of order; but the place was overrun by rabbits and the hunters were seldom exercised. Lady Cecilia gave me the freedom of the estate, told me I was to shoot where and when I pleased, and that the horses were mine to ride whenever I wished.

This kind of privilege soon becomes known, and it was not long before I received hints that the occasional visiting War Office dignitary would appreciate a day's shooting. Experience, however, taught me to be cautiously selective in my choice of guests. I preferred my own company around the estate.

I had never owned a shotgun, so I borrowed a small calibre rifle, a .22, from the armoury. It was a weapon used for target practice and could fire only one bullet without reloading, but I was a good shot and it was effective against rabbits. Long ago my luggage had been reduced to a bare minimum. Tweed jacket and flannels were at home in Scotland. In my battle dress, with the rifle slung over my shoulder, I didn't present the picture of a country gentleman as I wandered through the woods.

The padre, who told me he had many times shot grouse on the Scottish moors, hinted that he would like to accompany me some time, and with vague assurances that one day I would take him with me, I went about my duties. These took me to the local hospital, and it was no surprise one day to meet our spiritual adviser in one of the hospital corridors.

As we stood chatting, I heard someone singing, and round the corner came a vivacious student nurse. She was a black-eyed Susan, that girl — pretty, shapely and perpetually cheerful. With her dark hair, the blue and white uniform that hid enough of her figure to make the rest tantalizing, the ridiculous nurse's cap perched on the top of her head, she would have tempted a Renoir to reach for his easel. I had had dealings with her over patients we sent in. She cheered their days for them. She was a perky, warm little urchin of a thing, her unabashed north-country accent only emphasizing her liveliness. At eighteen, she was an excellent student nurse.

She saw us, and if the singing ceased abruptly, her smile did not. She waved and went on her bright and busy way.

"A cheerful little songbird!"

It was the padre speaking, as his gaze followed her down the corridor. He turned to me and, half smiling, asked, "Where was I now, when we were interrupted?"

Weeks passed and I was too busy either to canter the hunters or tramp through the woods, but the padre reminded me of my promise, and I arranged to meet him one Saturday morning in a few weeks' time.

My rounds took me far afield. Then one day, in the dining room of a country hotel, I saw him again. Deep in conversation with him, eyes fixed upon his face in rapt attention, was our little nurse. Unnoticed, I ate my meal and went on my way. Next morning I met the padre at headquarters.

"Did you enjoy your meal, Doctor? A nice spot, the Blue Heron, I always think!"

"Yes," I answered. "Yesterday, of course...yes, a nice place."

If I felt embarrassed, my voice was casual, but the padre was completely at ease as he went on. "She's a nice little thing, don't you think?"

"Yes, she is, and a jolly good nurse, too."

"I'm sure of that, Doctor. Her other attributes are equally fetching, I would say."

This wasn't quite the line I had expected, and I eyed the padre askance, but his bland expression hadn't changed.

"In fact," he went on, "I intend to bed her before I leave here."

I was shocked! I stared at him and exploded, "She's a child, man — eighteen! You've got daughters her age!"

"And what," he asked evenly, "has that got to do with it? Juliet was probably fourteen."

"Romeo wasn't on the wrong side of forty-five with a wife and children," I snapped.

"You're not attracted to the girl yourself, by any chance, are you, Doctor — or are you?"

"No, I'm not!" I snapped back. "I just don't approve of what you're saying."

The padre smiled. "If you knew a little more of psychology and a little less about medicine, you might have more understanding of human nature, my friend. If you ask me, you're probably a fool where women are concerned," he added gratuitously.

And he was gone.

A few weeks passed before we met again, and then one Saturday morning he appeared in my office as I was completing a report. There he stood, dressed in a tweed jacket, sweater and corduroy trousers. With his game bag slung over his shoulder, shotgun couched over the crook of his left arm, contentedly puffing at his pipe, he was the very picture of an English country gentleman.

"May I sit, Doctor?"

I had grown a little cool towards the padre, but remembering my promise to take him shooting, I nodded towards the one chair gracing the cubbyhole that was my office.

"We were going shooting together. Remember?"

"Yes. I'll be with you in a moment."

The report was completed. I signed it, threw it into the tray and walked towards the cupboard where I kept my borrowed rifle, but stopped to answer the telephone. Turning, I saw my colleague's composed smile as he watched me. Putting the telephone down, I asked, "Is something amusing you?"

"I suppose you could say that," he replied. "I thought you might be interested to know I've made a woman of our friend."

"I see."

"Last night. An experience she will remember," he said, walking over to my desk and emptying the contents of his pipe in an ashtray. "And now, shall we go?"

"You weren't in love with that girl," I said coldly, "and I don't believe you gave a damn about her."

"I never said I did."

"Will you be seeing her again?"

"No. That would be poor tactics." He looked at me appraisingly. "You're angry, of course. Probably jealous. You found her attractive, did you not? Under your Presbyterian inhibitions, you, my friend, are jealous."

"I'm not a moralist," I retorted, "but for me, going to bed with someone would have to mean something." And yet a small voice within me hinted that he perhaps was right.

As if reading my thoughts, he said affably, "Love, I suppose?"

"Yes," I replied, lamely. "Love."

"Love," he smiled. "Ah! Love!" he repeated mockingly. "Physical need and chemical attraction, if you're talking of sex — which, after all, Doctor, is quite a different thing!"

I was getting rattled. "Well," I asked in one final effort to remain dispassionate, "what about your calling, the question of scruples? You're a man of the cloth!"

"You're talking like a Scotch temperance lecturer," he replied.

His controlled smile was beginning to infuriate me. And then he added, disparagingly, "You do realize, don't you, that she's a working-class girl? That makes quite a difference, you know. And as for rules, my friend," he concluded, "remember that rules were made to be broken."

Without a word I picked up my rifle and led the way. Once on the estate, I tramped through my favourite copse to the large meadow.

"Go that way," I indicated gruffly, "and I'll take this side."

He walked off, loaded shotgun under his arm.

I was glad to be on my own. A lot of what he said had hit home. John Knox's Calvinism has eaten into the very bones of too many Scots. For many of us, sex is synonymous with sin and guilt. But it was his cool smugness about the whole affair, his amused appraisal of my reaction, that riled me. At the same time I could see the cold logic of many of his remarks. Didn't anything get under the man's skin? Obviously not, I thought, as I walked across the stubble.

He had walked a little distance when I saw, about fifty yards straight ahead of me, a cock pheasant taking a morning stroll. It stood for a second or two, took a tentative step preparatory to takeoff, hesitated, then stood still. I raised my rifle and kept the bird in my open sights. It was a shot for a marksman, but then, that's what I was. It was wartime. Army rations were adequate, but not much fun. Temptation got the better of me. Gently, I squeezed the trigger. The bullet sped to its mark, and there, in a puff of feathers, lay supper.

There was a shout from my left and the chaplain came hurrying towards me, gesticulating, shouting something. He broke into a half run. As he drew near, I saw the clenched fist waving at me. His face was suffused with anger.

"By God, I saw that, you know," he roared. "Saw the whole thing. It's not done, sir. It's simply not done! By God, sir, you shot that bird on the ground!"

Chapter Eighteen

The war years were the zenith of some men's lives. Others were broken by war.

Its heroes, of whom I was never one, returned to a land unfit for them. In Britain, on demobilization, they simply went back into uniforms called demob suits of blue, grey or brown that could be spotted a block away for what they were. And then, facing into a colourless, exhausted world, they went back, as like as not, to their old jobs.

Janet and I, though we had been married for five years, had never lived together for any length of time. We were nearly thirty. We had both changed. In some ways we had to find one another again. And we had a little daughter of three who was bewildered by this strange man who called himself Daddy.

We were lucky. Like most of our friends we had no money, but we were doctors and there was work for doctors to do. We borrowed a few hundred pounds and bought a practice in the city of Hull, on the Humber estuary in Yorkshire on the northeast coast of England.

Hull, with about a quarter of a million people in the general area, was Britain's third seaport. During the war its docks had been of immense importance and hence it had been a constant target for enemy bombers, sustaining more damage than Coventry. The lists of dead and injured ran into the thousands and Hull's people were worn out mentally and physically.

The practice we bought had been unattended for six years. The doctor who owned it had joined the army at the beginning of the war, had been deafened by gunfire and was unable to hear his patients talk to him. He was only too happy to sell us what he believed to be a lost cause, and sold what had once been a flourishing practice at a fire-sale price. His misfortune became our good fortune, for within a year people began to return to their homes and soon we had as many patients as we could properly care for.

Our office was adjacent to areas that had suffered heavy damage, and one of the first responsibilities was to give moral support to people whose nervous systems had become exhausted. Many came to the surgery suffering from strange symptoms that fitted into no recognizable pattern of disease.

Careful physical examination and reassurance often worked wonders, and the time we spent in talking to people was seldom wasted, for tragedy was all around us. Hull was then one of the greatest deep-sea fishing ports in the world. Its seamen were famous even in the Middle Ages and their contribution to Britain's naval might has always been immense. That knowledge, however, is small consolation to a seaman's widow who has three little ones to raise. And we saw many such cases.

Janet had spent most of the war years working as a doctor in hospital and, though Catriona was born in 1943, she continued with her work. Doing so gave her a home and allowed her to employ a nanny. Her experience and skills far surpassed mine, but she had never managed a practice and a house at one and the same time, nor had she employed household help. And this she had to do. Cooking meals was another problem. For years her food had been prepared in hospital kitchens. Doctors, in scarce supply in hospitals, worked very long hours and there was little time to develop culinary skills.

Then there was me. I had become accustomed to wielding authority, and perhaps in my military way might have thought that Janet (with some training from me, of course) would have made a good junior officer. I must say I was speedily disabused of any notions I had in that direction!

Then there was our home. It had been badly damaged during the bombing. Fireplaces had been blasted into the middles of rooms. Ceilings had fallen down, windows had been shattered and boarded up. The place hadn't been lived in for six years, except by mice, and they were everywhere. However, the city authorities, anxious to have doctors in the area, made repairs swiftly and effectively — usually.

Just after dinner one night, the dining room ceiling, giving one sudden, despairing groan, crashed down, smashing crockery and ruining weeks of cleaning and polishing. Since the original ceiling had been made of heavy plaster, it was a miracle that no one's skull was smashed. The workmen moved in very quickly and effected repairs that have lasted for forty years.

We prospered. Our practice grew by leaps and bounds. Neighbouring doctors, mostly older men, were friendly and helpful, glad to see a couple of young physicians come to the area and relieve them of some of the heavy burden of work they had had to carry during the war.

Then came growing demands for a comprehensive health service. The deficiencies of the existing system — and those were very real — were constantly brought to the attention of the public. There was dissension among doctors, but on a recorded vote roughly half of Britain's doctors voted in favour of the legislation. And yet doctors as a group continued to be depicted as being stubbornly, even vehemently, opposed to changes that would ensure "free" and adequate medical care for all.

Janet, being a liberated woman and a social democrat, did not hesitate to speak in support of a national health service at public meetings. While I believed it was immoral to deny anyone necessary medical care for any reason, I had my doubts about the proposed scheme. It could be a splendid political football.

Despite a future that seemed increasingly uncertain, we kept working hard and our practice kept growing. Gradually our bomb-damaged, draughty old house became a comfortable home.

The National Health Service became law and the world did not come to an end. For a few years my fears seemed to be delusions.

Doctors accepted the terms and conditions of service and kept on working as before — well, perhaps not quite as before. Their work loads began to increase. House calls were now "free," so there were more of them, unfortunately, often for trifling reasons. Medications such as headache pills were free; so was cotton wool. The office sessions became busier. Not that the extra work benefited the doctors in any way. They were paid so many shillings per head per year regardless of the work done.

Janet's idealism as a social democrat was one day overwhelmed by her feelings as an outraged physician.

She had made an appointment at a hairdresser's, and heard one of the customers say to one of the women who worked there, "What's all the hurry with you?"

"Oh!" replied the hairdresser, "I've an appointment with my doctor this afternoon."

"D'you mean to tell me you go to your doctor any more? Send for him to come to you! He's bound to do it. If he doesn't, just report him. Don't waste your time going to any doctor's surgery."

Nor did I react politely one evening when a man made himself comfortable at my desk and said: "I'll have a sick note, Doc. For a week."

"What's the matter?"

"Ankle, Doc — strained it at work."

"I'd better have a look."

"No. No need. Just the sick note."

"Well," I said, "I'm sorry, but if you want a sick note I have to examine your ankle. Besides, we may need an X-ray."

"Look, Doc, I don't need any examination. Just give me a sick note."

"Just as soon as I've examined you!"

"Doc," my patient's tone of voice hovered between being confidential and threatening, "I'm a shop steward in our union. You've a lot of our chaps 'ere an' if I doan't get that bloody note..."

I was halfway to opening the door by that time and the consultation came to an abrupt halt.

The vast majority of our patients were kindly, considerate and grateful, but incidents like this rankled, and somehow, it seemed, doctors — especially general practitioners — were often depicted as less than competent and sometimes uncaring. I felt that my own standard of work was deteriorating.

Young specialists, highly qualified after years of training, saw little chance of promotion and the exodus of doctors began. In the 1950s and 1960s, thousands of doctors left Britain until the government became concerned enough to set up a commission of enquiry.

We had security, but with it a growing sense of frustration. We took what steps we could to improve matters. That genial and compatible character, Dr. Gilbert Swanson, joined us, becoming as much a friend as an associate.

We said good-by to the old house and bought a new house in the village of West Ella, a few miles from the surgery. We were no longer at the beck and call of any passerby who decided he "just wanted a word or two with the doctor."

With the lawns, rose garden and copse of trees, it was Janet's dream house come true. But even this did not calm my growing frustration and determination to leave the National Health Service.

In the spring of 1955, after a family conference in which Catriona, a quiet, wise little girl of eleven, took part, the die was cast. We decided to emigrate to Canada.

When we left a few months later, Janet looked back at her beloved home and said prophetically, "Darling, I don't know what the future holds for us, but one thing I do know. I'll never ever have a house like that again."

Chapter Nineteen

In emigrating we had thrown security to the winds. That kind of decision is never easy. It was not made easier by Britain's decision in the hard times of the period to freeze the funds of people leaving the country. Our savings had to stay in the frozen sterling funds. Even my life insurance policy could be collected only in Britain.

We knew nothing of Canada's West other than what we had read, but the Canadian immigration authorities had given us the names of three small towns that needed doctors. It was Janet who chose Okotoks because, she said with irrefutable logic, the name had two OKs in it and it was "bound to be all right."

Airplanes have effected great changes in travel. There is none of the physical and mental adjustment today that used to accompany travel by sea and rail when that was "the only way to go." Even by travelling in one of the older propeller-driven planes then in use, it took us only two days to reach Alberta and the little town of Okotoks with its seven hundred people, its wooden houses and gravelled roads. It was another world to us.

Although it was the beginning of June, the grass lay limp, dank and yellow by the roadside ditches. Here and there in hollows in the ground lay patches of greyish-white snow, untouched by the early summer sun. It had been a long, hard winter and the earth seemed still to be defying the warmer weather. The sun's rays drenched the streets and the countryside by day, but the evenings were cold. It was the sun and the blue skies of the Canadian West that made those early, anxious days so bearable.

The immigration authorities had told us they would notify the town of our intention to settle there, but when we arrived we might have been creatures from outer space. Nobody had heard of us and at first nobody seemed very interested either. In a state of shock, I told Janet that if someone had landed a rickety old biplane in the main street and offered to fly us back to England, I'd have been tempted to accept!

But despair soon evaporated. George Lock, the mayor, Frank Pow, the bank manager, Jack Meston, the real estate agent, and others descended on our hotel room, asked us to give them a few days and assured us something would be done, for, they said, the town "sure needed a doctor."

Calgary, a city of 150,000, lay twenty-five miles to the north, and the nearest town with a hospital, High River, lay fifteen miles to the south. In the winter, when roads became blocked by snow, a doctor in the town would be a blessing, they said. Sometimes it was impossible to leave the place when the Mounted Police put barriers across the road, for in blizzards people could die of exposure even in their cars. Stay, they said. It was unfortunate that they hadn't been told of our coming, but we mustn't worry. They were happy to see us, and something would be done.

Indeed, something was done. Mr. Pow of the Royal Bank lent me $2,000, saying it was an investment, not a loan, and Mr. Meston found us a house. It wasn't much of a house, perhaps. I'm told it had once been two small settlers' homes joined together. It wasn't insulated and the basement was an earth dugout containing the plumbing and heating equipment. There were two small bedrooms, a living room and kitchen equipped with an old wood stove converted to coal — a far cry from Janet's modern, streamlined Aga cooker at Hull, but that house became home for a year, and we made the most of it.

There wasn't an office of any kind available in Okotoks, and so we practised from the kitchen for several months until we bought the Skye Glen schoolhouse. We found it lying deserted in a field outside town. It was part of the short history of the West. It had been a one-room school where young ladies, hardly older than the students they taught, had brought education to the region.

We weren't pioneers, but I sometimes thought we were the next best thing, what with our earth dugout for a basement and the sight of that old, grey, wooden building with a few ancient wood-and-steel school desks in it still, standing forlorn and worn. But volunteers hauled the schoolhouse into town, set it up on a cement foundation, and soon it was painted, divided into consulting and waiting rooms and made ready for business...which at first didn't materialize. I almost accepted a splendid offer — jobs for both of us and a house in Regina, Saskatchewan, four hundred miles to the east.

It was the Welcome Wagon that made me change my mind; that and the warmth of the townsfolk.

Having nothing to do one morning, I decided to explore the town, and on my way home was just in time to intercept two ladies trying to manoeuvre a large, heavily laden trolley through the garden gate into our cottage.

"Good morning," I greeted them. "I'm afraid you've made some mistake. My name is Gibson and this is the house we live in."

"No indeed, Doctor," said Mrs. Waldron, introducing herself and her companion. "You see, this is an old custom of the West. This is the Welcome Wagon. In the early days, people contributed something of their own to all new settlers and we still keep up the custom. This is still the West and this is the "welcome" wagon for our new doctors, the Gibsons."

That Welcome Wagon was the beginning. We had arrived carrying only our flight bags. Our "settlers' effects," as they were still romantically labelled in the bill of lading, would follow us by sea and rail and should arrive within a month. It took four months. We were notified that a dock strike in England had delayed their transportation, and the Welcome Wagon simply grew at an amazing rate. We had offers of curtains, chairs and even a bed until our effects arrived.

All the same, people were chary of us at first. They wondered why we had come to such a small town. Calgary was growing fast, and some folks later told me it was difficult to realize that we actually wanted to settle in a small place when the city with all its amenities was so close. And I've often wondered, though nobody said it, if they thought we couldn't have been too smart, and so settled for a small town rather than compete in a large one!

I do know this. Immigrants who went straight to large cities may have prospered, but they could not have known, as we did, the joys of living in the countryside. And perhaps they never discovered the Canada we came to know and love.

Since we had few patients in those early months, we explored the countryside. For a few hundred dollars I bought a secondhand Chevvy. It was years old, worn and chipped, but it was reliable and I kept it for five years. It carried us many a mile.

Okotoks lay in a hollow, the valley of the Sheep River, protected from the steel-cold north winds of winter by a grassy, treeless ridge. To the south lay low mounds of hills that flowed into broad, fertile valleys. To the west lay the foothills, one undulating range after another, the light green of the grass interrupted in summer by the darker colour of the copses of aspen, and in winter the snow-covered ground contrasting with the light brown of brush and trees. And in serried ranks against the skyline, the unforgettable peaks of the Rockies, pink in the light of the rising sun; blue, grey and purple in the daylight; cold, dark and menacing at dusk.

To the east, only ten miles away, the prairie began, with roads crossing it — gravel roads that could stop the terrifying prairie fires that once destroyed everything in their path for maybe a hundred miles before they died out.

The prairie was fenced now, the land productive; the bison had gone. Indians no longer erected their tepees where they pleased, and I marvelled one evening as I stopped the car by the roadside, to think that all that was within living memory. I had met an old rancher who had seen the Indians on horseback in their warpaint, firing their rifles into the air and circling a column of red-coat policemen, as he called the men of the North-West Mounted Police, the forerunners of the Royal Canadian Mounted Police. The red-coats, he told me, had stayed silently watchful in their ranks, tolerating threats and insults until the Indians tired of it all and their chiefs parlayed with the officer in command.

The prairie, an undulating plain that stretches for hundreds of miles, has a beauty that is not always appreciated at first glance. The few scattered trees and brushland are all that break the monotony of the landscape, though here and there lie the lakes or ponds called sloughs, and these become beautiful as they reflect the pinks, scarlets and purples of the setting sun. And above it all, that great vault of sky that is the glory of the West.

Appreciation of the scenery is one thing; making a living another, and patients were slow to come to us. I became anxious. And yet Janet and I had our office on the main street by now. It lacked the sophistication of some city clinics, but it was efficiently equipped and we felt we could practise good medicine there. We had also been admitted as members of the staff of the High River Hospital fifteen miles away.

Still, one night when our little one was asleep we discussed our situation. We knew that there were openings for us in the city, but by now we had made friends in Okotoks. We loved its quietness. We enjoyed walking along the untamed banks of the river. We enjoyed rambling in the fields, listening to the distant, eerie howling of the coyotes in the quiet nights. We didn't want to move.

"But," said Janet, "they're just not used to women doctors. I'm not sure that anybody really wants to see me if you're in the office. Even the women are used to men doctors. And as for the men — they're such a macho lot."

It was a few weeks later that I was detained at the hospital. Janet had to tackle the office on her own and, strangely enough, if it wasn't exactly busy, it wasn't what you'd call quiet either, and she'd seen quite a few people.

I walked in just as Freddy Ostler walked out of Janet's consulting room. Now Freddy, I would say, is a macho type.

He greeted me as he passed.

"Hi, Doc! I hope you didn't mind my seeing your wife? I'm busy and I hadn't the time to wait. That okay with you?"

"Of course, Fred."

"Oh, good. D'you mind if I see her again?"

"No, Fred, of course not. It's all the one firm."

"Well, that's okay then. But don't you want to know why I wouldn't mind seeing her again?"

Since Fred obviously wanted to tell me, I humoured him.

"Sure, go ahead, Fred."

"Well, Doc, for one thing, she's prettier than you. An' for another, by God, I think she's smarter, too."

The partnership was back in action.

Chapter Twenty

The Stampede Ranch! The very name conjures up a vision of the West, and the Stampede Ranch typified the West. It had been owned in the early days by Guy Weadick, rancher, cowboy, impresario and one of the cofounders of the Calgary Stampede. His name is still famous in southern Alberta, associated with what is often billed as the Greatest Outdoor Show on Earth.

When we first visited the ranch in the summer of 1955 it was owned by Mrs. Ruby Lee and her brother, Dick Machin. They had both lost their partners in life and had joined forces to buy the ranch, situated in wooded hill country close to the first range of the Rockies.

The ranch house and the outbuildings, built of heavy logs painted white and edged with black, made an attractive foreground to the thickly forested hills that lay behind them. Ostensibly the place was a "dude ranch," as guest ranches are known to the locals in the West. Dick, however, still ran a herd of cattle, the paying guests being more or less a sideline. It was a far cry from some of the highly advertised commercial "outfits" in the United States that cater to paying guests.

Dick and Ruby were in their middle fifties when first we met them, and very soon our professional relationship became one of friendship. Most weekends Janet, Catriona and I drove that forty miles west of Okotoks through the small town of Black Diamond, south on that long, straight, bare road to the village of Longview and then west again into the foothills and the ranching country. We'd drive past the O.H. and the Buffalo Head ranches with the houses miles apart until we turned into the gate to our friends' place, driving over the grassy track on the meadow to the ranch house.

Ruby would be preparing lunch on the ranch house stove, the smell of freshly made bread and cookies mingling with the aroma of roast beef that had been cooked to perfection.

Dick might be talking to an early arrival (for some of the guests would have motored down from Calgary that morning) or he might be in the corral selecting the horses for the afternoon's riding, or superintending the hired hand as he saddled the animals. The horses, sensing the coming action, would be restless, whinnying, tossing their heads or pawing the ground in search of a blade or two of grass that had so far escaped notice.

Some guests would be standing around in the kitchen talking, stepping quickly out of Ruby's way as she moved about her chores. Others, in small groups in the sitting room, talked to one another. There would usually be about a dozen people there.

Dick, having settled matters to his satisfaction, would regale his audience with one of his hilarious and improbable stories that invariably proved verifiable. Laughter was always close at hand.

They were a happy lot, the guests. Mostly they were city people, but like most Albertans of thirty years ago their roots were in the land and often the men would step outside to help saddle the horses. They'd done that kind of work since they'd been youngsters and in their checked shirts, Stetsons, blue jeans and cowboy boots, they looked as if they'd never left the farm.

And then there was the "Major." He was a permanent resident who had lived at the ranch for years, renting one of the old bunkhouses. At the weekends he was always very correct. A stylish cravat — at least it had been stylish thirty years earlier — was worn with his very English open-neck shirt and grey flannel trousers.

In summer, as I recall, he'd occasionally wear an ancient Panama hat and in winter a cloth cap. The British Army had left an indelible stamp on him. With his upper-class English accent, his military moustache and his frequent references to military matters, he was a figure of Empire — a somewhat tarnished figure perhaps, but of Empire all the same. I was invited once or twice to visit him in his bunkhouse. Tidiness was not his greatest virtue. He could have done with a bit of help from his long-departed batman.

When he discovered I'd been a military man myself, there was no stopping him. Although he had left the army in the 1920s, his memory for events of long ago was prodigious and his dissertations were lengthy. He kept reminding me that he'd "had a Staff job, y'know," and once he got going, he could be a bit of a bore. I really wasn't very interested in the strategies that led to the downfall of Kut, nor was I intrigued by the 1916 railway transport arrangements for taking troops from Calais to the front. Nevertheless, he had a fund of stories about the flamboyant characters he'd met in the West when he first came to Canada. All in all he was an unusual character to find living as a semirecluse on a ranch.

One Sunday, Ruby and Dick told us they now considered us to be their friends, and refused to accept any payment from us for all their hospitality. That connotation placed us in quite a different position from the guests, who paid for lunch and the riding that followed it. And what modest payment it was! They were insistent that we should come regularly.

Weekend lunches were convivial affairs, with the food plentiful and superb, and Ruby the perfect hostess. Seated at the large circular ranch tables, with the Lazy Susans in the middle, it was easy to strike up conversations. The Lazy Susans were old ranch cart wheels adapted to rotate at the merest touch, carrying bread, vegetables, meat and condiments to whomever required them.

The conversation might not have suited Canada's intellectual elite, but it certainly sparkled. Oil and cattle often led the subjects for discussion, but politics had its place. Dick often acted as "moderator," with just that touch of humorous cynicism that kept the conversation flowing.

It was at one such lunch some months after our promotion from "guests" to "friends" that the lady sitting next to me abruptly enquired, "Are you a guest or a friend?"

I was a little taken aback, but as her question was put to me in a most good-humoured way, I answered that I was a friend.

Both Dick and Ruby had left the room for a few minutes, and my neighbour put the same question to the person sitting on her other side. He also, it transpired, was a friend.

"D'you know," said my questioner, "I just wonder how many people here actually are paying guests, and how many are friends."

It took a hurried minute before Ruby's return with a large dish of steaming potatoes to ascertain that all twelve of us having lunch there that day were friends.

That was typical of the co-owners of the Stampede Ranch, where for many years we found a haven from the varied crises with which the country doctor has to contend.

Chapter Twenty-one

When we visited or stayed at the Stampede Ranch, we were over forty miles from our office and almost as far from the hospital at High River. But we were within instant reach by telephone, even if our house was empty and our telephone unattended.

Certainly we were within our parish boundaries, so to speak. Neighbouring ranchers were our patients, and even though our headquarters were so far away, we could be reached instantly.

What a debt we owed to the Okotoks telephone operators. They were housed in a small building on the main business street and for years they were among our greatest allies. We will never forget them.

Gradually our practice grew, and in a countryside so sparsely populated compared with most parts of rural England, sickness could bring great anxiety, especially to parents. The telephone service was a godsend at such times. When there were accidents, neighbours could quickly be summoned to help, perhaps to drive injured people to hospital, and that link with the local doctor was all-important. We felt a sense of personal loss when eventually the operators were replaced by an automatic exchange.

We had operators for years, though we used to call them "the telephone girls." Some of them weren't "girls" any longer — they were married women, single ladies or widows, and they were constantly helpful. They made life easy for us when it could have been very difficult. Their cheerful co-operation saved our time and eased our responsibilities. They had, for example, an uncanny knack for tracking us down in an emergency. They knew that we lunched in Calgary's Palliser Hotel on our weekly half-day. They knew we'd be at the Willumsens' place or the Stampede Ranch at the weekends, and they also knew we had a habit of dropping in on our friends and namesakes, the Gibsons, for a chat after our afternoon office sessions in Okotoks.

They kept that information to themselves, but when we were needed that phone would ring wherever we were and our friends would say, "It'll be for one of you two."

And it generally was. But the operators used their discretion and we were seldom disturbed for trifles. I'm sure that half the countryside realized that the "phone girls" knew where we were, but people seldom abused that little service, provided so courteously and gratuitously by our rural telephone operators of twenty and thirty years ago. Sometimes, patients would discuss their problems briefly with the operator and a consensus would be arrived at as to whether or not the occasion warranted disturbing either of the doctors!

Parents twenty or thirty miles away in lonely farms west of Turner Valley or Millarville could become very worried about signs of illness in their children, especially in the evenings as darkness closed in and perhaps heavy snow began to fall. Janet was an expert adviser in such cases, either by reassuring parents or advising them that immediate attention was advisable. The women relied on her immensely and it wasn't unusual for me to pick up the phone to be greeted with a voice saying, "Doctor, would you mind if I spoke to Dr. Janet for a minute? I've got a sick little girl here and I thought if I could just have a word with her..."

Several families would share a party line. It would be two long and two short rings for the Smiths, two longs for the Joneses and three shorts for the MacTavishes, and soon everybody who shared a party line knew who was being telephoned.

"That's for the Muirs," somebody would say as the old-fashioned box telephone on the wall gave one short and one long ring. "It's not for us."

The party line system had a funny side to it as well.

One evening two women we knew were having a heated discussion when a silent listener, outraged, unable to contain herself one moment longer, broke into the conversation and contradicted them both.

One little boy who was very attached to Janet brought her stories and verbatim conversations that could amuse, alarm and horrify her. The youngster was usually totally innocent of the import of some of the things he'd overheard. With his parents at work, alone on the out-skirts of town with neither a television set nor a radio in the house, rubber-necking, as eavesdropping was called, was his only and very innocent entertainment.

It wasn't always so innocent. Late one night, half asleep, I answered our telephone's insistent ringing. Like most townspeople we had a private telephone. As soon as I lifted the receiver I knew it was a call from the country. I seemed to be hearing a voice from the middle of the Sahara.

"Can you speak louder?" I bellowed.

"I'm trying, Doctor," that disembodied voice replied.

"Just a minute," I yelled and jingled the receiver handle, a manoeuvre that brought an instant response from the operator.

"Are you having troubles, Doctor?"

"Helen," I replied, "this is a terrible line. Can you do something for me? I can't hear a thing!"

"Doctor," said Helen's sweetly feminine voice, "there's nothing wrong with the line. But if half the goddamn neighbours would hang up their receivers you'd hear just fine."

An immediate series of clicks signified that Helen's diagnosis had been correct. A late night phone call, however, often meant trouble and as like as not the listeners were wondering if help was needed.

But we agreed that we'd come to a very open society!

Chapter Twenty-two

"I've been invited to a pow-wow," said our friend, "and so have you and Janet and Catriona — tomorrow night. We'll go in my car, and I'll pick you up."

It was the winter of 1955, one of the coldest on record. It had snowed for days, but now the air was still, the skies clear and quiet. The cold was so intense that the wooden beams in the roof of our house contracted and cracked as though they would break. It was not the kind of weather for travel. Still, pow-wows are private affairs to which white people are seldom invited or welcomed, and a forty- or fifty-mile trip to the reserve seemed a small price to pay for such an experience.

It was dark when our neighbour's car drew up at our gate that night. Warmly clad, we set out. The Indians were old friends of his, and he esteemed their friendship.

"This will be a real pow-wow," he told us. "They'll be talking mostly in their own language. There'll be a speech or two from the old chiefs — they still have a lot of authority, you know. It should be interesting."

We drove twenty miles to Black Diamond, then south on the undulating road to Longview. Huge flares burning excess natural gas cast strange, flickering lights and shadows over the bare hillsides for miles, before we turned west once again into cattle country. It was dark by now and quiet as we drove along the lonely road past the Stampede Ranch, then across the bridge on the Sheep River and into the reserve.

Unpainted houses and shacks, with rusting old motorcars nearby, were scattered about in a disorderly sort of way, for a liking for town planning is no part of the Indian culture.

"We're going to Brown Eagle's place for a cup of tea," announced our friend, drawing up at the door of a wooden hut. We were ushered in. The smell of buckskin was everywhere. Mrs. Eagle, a tall, pleasant-looking, middle-aged woman with the olive complexion and dark braids so typical of her race, shyly bade us welcome. She wore moccasins with buckskin leggings and slipped quietly about her chores, too diffident to be drawn into conversation, though her smiles made it plain that we were welcome in her home.

This was a one-room wooden structure with a heavy iron wood stove for heating. Three brass bedsteads stood against the walls, a wooden table occupied the middle of the carpetless floor, a kitchen chair stood by the stove, and cooking utensils lay on the floor. The wooden walls were bare of decoration, the windows uncurtained. But the house was neatly kept. It was the home of simple people with simple needs; and there was an unaffected dignity there, too, as the Eagles courteously waited for us to finish our tea.

Mr. Eagle left before us to tell of our arrival, and soon we were on our way to the meeting hall, driving through snow between the trees standing stark and still, silhouetted against the night sky. Just ahead of us, a young man cantered along on horseback to guide us on the trail.

Suddenly the car came to a stop. We were hub-deep in snow. Our neighbour, used to such conditions, climbed out, surveyed the situation and reassured us that we would be on our way as soon as we had "done some spade work and put chains on."

As we stood beside the car, a young Stony drove by in a "democrat," the once ubiquitous horse-drawn buggy of the prairies. Grinning, the youth reined in his horse and offered to take us to the community hall a few hundred yards away.

"Come in democrat," he invited us. "Car no good. Get stuck in snow anytime. Horse no get stuck in snow — an' no use smelly gas either! More fun to come with me!"

But we soon had the car moving and within a few minutes had reached the hall. We might have entered another era. Around the outside of the hall there were tethered several dozen horses, some saddled, some harnessed to democrats. The only motorcar in sight was our own, and how out of place it looked in *that* setting.

The Indian band is a community of several hundred people at most, of whom perhaps fifty or sixty were in the hall waiting for the pow-wow to begin. Our first impression was of a haze of tobacco smoke and that musty, pervasive smell of buckskin.

While the men, a husky, well-built lot, sat comfortably on benches on one side of the hall, puffing contentedly at their pipes and talking in a surprisingly animated sort of way, the women, on the opposite side of the hall, sat on the floor.

All conversation stopped abruptly when we appeared. Every eye was upon us as we were ushered to one end of the hall where a bench had been set aside for us. Catriona, as quiet as a mouse, sat between Janet and me, while our friend went over to talk to acquaintances — "visiting," as country folk say in the West.

An old man, obviously a person of authority, spoke to the gathering in their own language and immediately the silence was broken. Pipes were relit, men continued their interrupted conversations, and babies once again began to crawl about on the floor between the rows of women.

"Chief just tell them who you are," said the Indian who had guided us to our bench. He obviously meant to be our interpreter for the evening.

As he said that, friendly nods and smiles were directed at us from the benches. What a portrait painter's paradise confronted us! What faces! Some seemed incredibly old, deeply lined and wrinkled beyond belief, with eyes like black jewels. Some of the old people, we were told, could not speak a word of English.

The women sat silent. Here and there a papoose was strapped to a mother's back. Some of the girls were pretty, but that was diminished by their impassive expressions. Some of the older women wore buckskin dresses, the younger ones cotton frocks with patterned beadwork. All wore moccasins and buckskin leggings. There were three rows of women sitting cross-legged on the floor, with the babies now almost unheeded, crawling about. When one little rascal headed towards the men, however, he was hurriedly cuffed and yanked back into place.

The men talked affably, nodding genially towards us should glances cross, and there was a good deal of shuffling about as they made room for newcomers. One of them was obviously a personage. A middle-aged man, shabbily but decently dressed in blue jeans and jacket over a colour-ed shirt, he was accompanied with much courtesy to a special seat, his arrival greeted by a chorus of deep-throated grunts from the men.

"Councillor from another band," whispered our interpreter. "Pow-wow start now."

No sooner had he spoken than the chief who had introduced us rose to his feet and strode to and fro, addressing the gathering. He was the soul of eloquence. With that aquiline, proud old face, and the black braids falling over his shoulders, he was an impressive figure. His voice rose and fell in measured tones. His gestures had a calculated dignity. There were silences between declarations, and even the silences were eloquent, interrupted only by occasional grunts of obvious approval from the men. When he finished and sat down, there was much low-voiced exclamation, all of it respectful.

A younger man also spoke, but he was not as skilled a speaker as the chief, nor did he have the authority. The guest from Morley was the final speaker.

"Business over," whispered our interpreter. "Dancing start soon."

In the middle of the floor stood a large tom-tom. Four young men grouped themselves around it, the shadow of their Stetsons projected by the guttering lamps like giant witches' hats against the wall.

"We do Owl Dance now," said our interpreter. "You dance, too. You choose girl. Men come for your wife and daughter."

"Owl Dance!" I exclaimed. "I can't do your Owl Dance!"

"Easy — follow man in front," was the reply.

There was a low beat from the tom-tom. I asked a girl to partner me. Janet and Catriona had been asked to accompany a couple of young men and we fell into line, the men on the outside of the circle. The Owl Dance is not a deliriously wild affair. To me it is an animated shuffle, and my partner's face reflected the excitement of the occasion. Suddenly she began to giggle irrepressibly. Fearful that my partner might collapse from laughing at my efforts, I was quite happy to return to my seat and let her regain her composure. Obviously I was not going to become an Indian ballroom dance champion! Janet, I noticed, was making a lively attempt to enter into the spirit of the occasion, while our little one demurely followed the steps.

More dances followed. Courtesy demanded that I should attempt several of them, but it is only fair to say that Janet gave a better account of herself that evening than I did.

There was a pause. A consultation was held around the tom-tom. Heads were bent as the drummers beat the gentlest of tattoos. There was the softest tinkling of bells in the background; a door was opened and a group of six men entered. The youngest could not have been more than seven or eight, the oldest somewhere in his twenties. They were dressed in the ceremonial garb of Indian dancers.

They filed in quietly, one by one, pirouetting slowly in time with the soft beat of the tom-tom, the dozens of little bells sewn onto their costumes tinkling in time with their movements.

The audience watched the dancers intently as by the guttering light of kerosene lamps that cast weird and giant shadows on the walls they began to move in wider circles, following the intricate steps of the bell dance.

Their costumes of bright blues, greens and purples added to the exotic sight, with feathered headdresses swaying and weaving as the dancers circled. The smallest boy was dressed in a green, skintight suit, the bright plumage of his headdress contrasting with his dark skin, his face puckered in concentration as he followed the rhythm of the dance.

And there, too, was the "redskin" of fiction — young, lithe, thin-lipped, inscrutable, the bells on his ankle- and wristbands making hardly a sound as he moved slowly, deliberately round the drummers.

The beat of the tom-tom grew faster, louder. There was a high-pitched yell and the dance was on. The dancers whirled and stamped like creatures possessed. The ringing of the bells, once so quiet, became deafening. The tom-toms thundered in a strange, savage rhythm.

It went on for minutes, a hypnotic assault on the senses, the delirium of sound battering at one's brain till it reached an almost unbearable crescendo.

And then, suddenly, silence. The dancers slipped away.

It was early morning and time to leave. We thanked our hosts, and as we walked through the snow to our car, we could hear the distant howling of coyotes and see the aurora borealis swinging and crackling in that majestic curtain of colour in the sky far to the north.

I could see in my mind's eye that dignified old chief addressing his people. Although I had not understood a word of his speech, his measured eloquence had held me in its grip.

I could hear the bells, still ringing in my brain. And I remembered our last dance, a black-tie affair in Hull earlier that year.

It seemed a world — and a lifetime — away.

Chapter Twenty-three

It had been an honour, that invitation to a pow-wow. We had caught our first glimpse into the lives of Canada's Plains Indians, who are not necessarily similar in their ways or looks to other Canadian Indians.

We had seen how courtesy and dignity could survive in the midst of poverty. We had listened to an old chief speak with eloquence and authority and we had watched, absorbed, as young men demonstrated the intricate steps of their dances.

We were impressed. But we had seen only a façade. And our first glimpse of another reality was given to us as we drove home.

"I'm sorry I cut it a bit short," said our neighbour, "but it was over anyway. Just at the end there, I saw a bunch of young guys come into the hall. I could see they'd been drinking. They had a case of liquor with them. That's illegal. Liquor isn't allowed on reservations. It was time for us to go, believe me!"

"Why is it illegal for them to drink in their own homes?" I asked.

"Because," our neighbour replied curtly, "Indians don't hold their liquor like white men. I'll bet right now, despite the chief, they'll be drinking. In an hour they'll be quarrelling and in two, they'll be fighting, some of them, anyway."

"But you *like* Indians," I protested. "You've often said so. And some are your friends!"

"That's true," he replied. "There are a lot of fine people there, but liquor has been their downfall. And liquor was given them by white whisky traders in the first place," he added. "They didn't know anything about it until the whisky traders got to them. The North-West Mounted Police chased the traders out of the country, but their whisky stayed on.

I sat silently as our driver carefully steered the car through the deep snow. The only sound was the steady purr of the engine and the crunch of dry snow beneath our wheels. But distant lights glowing and fading in the sky meant that we were approaching the natural gas flares at Longview and the first habitation for miles.

Then Janet spoke. "I thought Mrs. Eagle was a very dignified lady," she said, "very handsome and very pleasant — but they have nothing, have they?"

"I guess you could say that," was the reply. "The old-timers had lots of dignity. But that went when they went. There are only a few old-timers left now."

I would learn a good deal more about Indians and their ways as the years went by. I could deal with them, often like them, but I question if I could ever understand them. And I question if many of them wanted to be understood.

They were never defeated in battle. They simply obeyed the white man's law. And they regarded the Mounted Police as their friends. The chiefs saw the demoralization wrought among their young people by liquor, and the North-West Mounted Police dealt sternly with the whisky traders. The police were their saviours. Commissioner J.F. Macleod of the Mounted Police was never known to break his word. Nor did Chief Crowfoot, when in 1877 he signed Treaty No. 7 with Macleod, accepting the sovereignty of Queen Victoria, "the Great White Mother" far away in London.

"If the police had not come to this country, where would we all be now?" asked Chief Crowfoot of his council. "Bad men and whisky were killing us so fast that few of us would have been left today."

Then he added with the kind of eloquence I had seen in that old chief at the pow-wow: "The police have protected us as the feathers of the bird protect it from the frosts of winter."

Thus war was avoided and the Indians moved into their allotted reservations: the Blackfoot, Bloods, Piegan, Sarcee and all the rest.

It's just over a hundred years since the Plains Indians were settled in reservations. They had been nomads, following the great buffalo herds upon which they had depended for food and clothing. They didn't know of the wheel. When they moved camp they pulled their belongings behind their horses, which they hitched to travois, two long poles trailing on the ground with a net between them to hold the load.

Yet they were a society, with chiefs and councils and societies of warriors and hunters. They had their medicine men who, though "not duly qualified," knew a thing or two, I am sure.

110

But liquor got to them and has stayed with them. Disease decimated them. Smallpox, tuberculosis and scarlet fever killed large numbers simply because, never having been in contact with such diseases, they had no immunity to them, and their bodily resistance was overwhelmed by the teeming bacteria.

Subsequently the survivors intermarried, not usually into other tribes, but among themselves, taking with them the genetic defects that the "noble savage" shares with the rest of mankind.

For instance, I know of one small interrelated band where many of its members, olive-skinned though they are, are acutely sensitive to sunlight, and this is very possibly a genetic defect that has proliferated because of intermarriage over the generations.

"But they can't hold their liquor like white men!" After a hundred years, surely innocence of liquor has worn off, and I have sometimes speculated that their inability to tolerate alcohol is also due to some ingrained genetic fault. After all, alcoholism as such can sometimes be determined genetically.

My mind, however, was not on medicine when one morning in the early spring of 1956, I drove towards Calgary from Claresholm, forty miles south of Okotoks. I was alone in the car and alone on the road, it seemed: that long, lonely, straight road that runs from Calgary to the U.S. border, 160 miles south.

Even as I do today, I wondered at the immensity of it all, with the flat, almost treeless prairie beginning by the roadside and stretching far into the eastern horizon. And to the west, fifty or sixty miles away, the jagged peaks of the Rockies etched against the sky.

And then I saw two people standing by the roadside, forlorn figures in that lonely landscape. As I drew near I recognized them as Indians, thumbing a ride. I slowed the car and drew up beside them. They were a young couple. The man wore blue jeans, a black, wide-brimmed Stetson much favoured by Indians, cowboy boots, checked shirt and a woollen windbreaker. His wife was dressed in a thin cotton frock over which she wore a buckskin jacket. Her legs were protected by buckskin leggings, and on her feet were moccasins, with rubber galoshes incongruously worn over them.

"Where to?" I asked.

"Calgary."

"In you get. I'm going to Calgary."

Without a word they climbed into the back seat of the car. The young man was a handsome, well set-up fellow, and his wife might have been pretty if only she had smiled.

I drove on with my passengers. Suddenly I felt sorry for them; sorry that their poverty made them hitch a ride on such a cold morning; sorry when I thought of their proud heritage, only a generation or two away. It was a far cry from the description once given me by an old rancher, when, as a young man, he'd seen the Indians come to Fort Macleod to parlay with the police.

"Proud as hell," he'd told me, "smelling of the grease they rubbed on their bodies. Their faces were smeared with paint, too, and they sure could ride. Arrogant as hell, too," he added.

And now, a generation or two later, hitching a ride from a passing motorist! I tried to strike up a conversation.

"So you're going to Calgary. Are you going to stay with friends?"

"Visit uncle."

Silence for miles. I tried again.

"You two are married?"

"Yes."

"Where do you come from?"

"Cardston."

"So you're Bloods?"

"Yes."

Another mile or two went by.

"Do you have any children?"

"One kid."

"Boy or girl?"

"Boy."

"Does he go to school?"

"Sometimes."

I expressed my hope that he would benefit from schooling and enlarged on the need of education in this day and age. Suddenly the floodgates were opened and the young man spoke.

"You right there. My kid going to get good education. Old chiefs no want that. They want to go back to old ways. Old ways gone forever. This a white man's world. My kid going to get white man's education."

It was quite a speech. He lapsed into silence and silence bore us company until we reached the outskirts of Calgary twenty miles farther on, where I let them out. The young woman had not uttered a word in forty miles, and they walked away without a word of thanks. I didn't feel they

112

owed me any, but I did think that better education might make the present-day Indian youngsters more communicative.

It was Bill Ross who put me to rights. He had had an education, and he was smart. A husky six-footer, Bill, with his broad, olive-skinned face and dark, flashing eyes was a handsome-looking character. What puzzled me was his name. The Clan Ross would have had difficulty in accepting Bill's right to wear their tartan, for he looked every inch a pure-blood Indian.

Knowing Bill a bit and appreciating his dry sense of humour, I said as much one day. Bill grinned when I said I found it difficult to believe that he was part white.

"I'm not part white, Doc. I'm a pure-blood Indian."

"But how come your name is Ross?"

"Oh! That's only my English name, Doc."

"Do you have another name?"

"Sure. Two more."

"How does that come about?"

"Well, you see, after you're born your mother might call you after something she sees. Like Running Rabbit, or Red Fox, or Long Knife, see?"

"I see. Very interesting."

"And then your uncle maybe give you a name, too. Lots of names."

"But, Bill, how the devil did you get the name Ross?"

"Oh. That's easy. My granddad was in the line-up when my tribe was registering. This old English bugger couldn't pronounce his name, so he gave him his own — Ross. That's how I got my English name."

"Ross isn't an English name," I said, somewhat tartly, "it's a Scottish name."

"Well then," said Bill with a grin, "it was an old Scotch bugger, wasn't it?"

"Bill," I said, "you may have solved a problem, you know. I've always wondered why so many chaps who look the real McCoy — full-blood Indians like yourself — have names like McLeod and McNeil. And there's the answer! Their names were given to them by Scotsmen. You know," I said, "the Scots are known all over the world for their moral rectitude..."

"Eh?"

"No playing around with the girls, Bill. That explanation has just saved the reputation of my fellow countrymen, eased my mind about something that has always worried me — all those Indians called Macpherson and the like — and it's all been perfectly innocent.''

"I'm happy for you, Doc," said Bill. "Happy to see you happy about it. All the same," he went on, "the way I have it, in the early days there were a lot of little Scotchmen going around this country on fast horses!''

Chapter Twenty-four

In many ways 1956 was a momentous year for us. In that year we had time to analyze our thoughts. We had experienced warmth and friendship from people in the town, where we felt we were both wanted and needed. After years away from hospital work I had risen to the challenge of being a hospital doctor once again, and I said to Janet on one occasion, "It's a poor day when I haven't learned something."

And we had come to the conclusion that the attractions of practice in the city could not compete with working in the country. So we decided to stay in our town in the foothills.

We managed to retrieve some of our savings from England and used the money to build a house, high on a bluff overlooking the town and the valley of the Sheep River, with a view of the mountains far away in the west.

Jack Brown, a local carpenter, who apologetically told Janet he'd built a lot of hencoops and a barn or two but never a house, undertook to build our new home. In his laconic and humorous way he expressed his fears that the task might be too much for him; he wondered about walls being blown over in the first winter storm, but with loving care and absolute integrity in his dealings with us, he built a house that could have withstood an earthquake.

Our new home became "the house that Jack built," or, to paraphrase the song, "our plywood bungalow in the West." It was to be a happy, lively home for years to come. And it would be witness, too, to strange and sometimes sad events, for with the nearest hospital fifteen miles away, people often arrived at our door in dire straits, desperate for help.

Eventually, to cope with inevitable emergencies, we furnished a small room in the basement of our new home as an emergency office. And over the years it was put to good use.

Catriona had settled in at the Okotoks High School with surprising ease. Despite having attended a girls' school in England, she soon found herself at ease with the local youngsters, making friends with a number of them, especially Mary Rowan, whose family became our friends and patients.

The Rowans owned a farm some miles from town, but catastrophe struck when, in one of those subtropical storms for which the prairies are notorious, lightning partially demolished what had been a comfortable farmhouse. Soon afterwards, Mrs. Rowan had to go into hospital for care and the treatment of recurrent cancer. Mary came to stay with us, and when her mother died, as our little daughter said, she "joined the team," calling our house her home. The two girls became inseparable companions. Passable horses were quite cheap to buy, and for two hundred dollars we bought two that next year — Peanuts, a four-year-old sorrel gelding for Catriona, and Gray, a part-Arab mare, for Mary.

Without doubt they soon were among the best groomed, most carefully kept animals in the whole of that valley. My use of the word pampered was indignantly censured by the two girls, who adored their horses but trained them, too. Our front lawn, a large patch of prairie, was ideal for "figure eights", and after school most days, training sessions were held. It was all taken very seriously!

I was kindly allowed to ride Peanuts, so called because that's what we paid for him. I was happy to leave Gray alone most of the time. She had some very unladylike habits. She was very fast in more ways than one, and had a knack, given the least opportunity, of nipping her rider, preferably in the seat of the pants, though anywhere else would do. Peanuts, on the other hand, was the most affable of characters, loving attention and responding to any show of affection. He would, if he was in the mood, trot towards Catriona or me in answer to our calls, though he usually preferred to play hard-to-catch until he allowed himself to be haltered.

Our practice began to grow. Janet's office sessions were held in the afternoons while the girls were at school. Her evenings were reserved for the supervision of homework. Mine were reserved for whatever might turn up, and the variety of work was amazing, ranging from cuts and bleeding noses sustained in ice hockey matches to broken bones sustained in falls from horses, to deadly heart attacks. There was no point, as had been the case in England, in referring such cases to the nearest hospital, for within the limits of our skills we all treated our own cases in hospital or else transferred patients to Calgary hospitals.

This took time, and since treatment often had to be given immediately, I became an earnest student of textbooks on emergency treatment.

Still, the challenge was immensely stimulating, and even if we didn't feel we were on our way to becoming millionaires, the rewards were adequate for us financially. In terms of gratitude and friendship, they were often heartwarming. Of course I made mistakes in that year, just as I sometimes made wrong decisions. Fortunately, all were rectified or rectifiable. Nobody suffered any permanent damage, and the thought that I might be sued for some error in judgement never entered my head. It was a very happy time to live in Canada, which was to many of us immigrants the land of the free — the land of opportunity. It is still that, of course, but over the years we as a nation have become more regulated, more controlled. That is in part because we have come to expect more from governments, and there is a price to be paid.

But in the West our friends and patients were the sons and daughters of the original settlers — British, American, European — and the spirit of independence was very strong. The West was opening up, with oil becoming as important as cattle.

There was a tremendously refreshing spirit of optimism in the air in those days. It was very infectious. Your neighbours were your friends. What affected them affected you. In the spirit of the old West, doors even in the town were often left unlocked so that passing friends from the country might find shelter or make a cup of tea. A sick farmer would find his fields harvested by his neighbours working as a team. A house partially destroyed by fire would be repaired by fellow townsmen, and clothes, shelter and food donated by the women. That was still the spirit of the West in 1956, and you could feel it.

And we learned something about the history of the West. Our next-door neighbour, a dignified old lady with a tremendous sense of fun, had been the first white girl to come to that part of southern Alberta. In the summer of 1883 her family arrived by Red River cart at the Gladys Ridge, just east of Okotoks, after a journey of eight hundred miles across the almost trackless prairies. As a little girl, Catherine Hogge had ridden most of the way. They spent the winter of 1883 in a tent, or rather in one tent inside another, the walls banked with straw and frozen snow against the cold blast of winter.

I stood talking to an elderly farmer one day and admired his prosperous-looking farmhouse and well-kept fields.

"How did you come to choose this land?" I asked.

"Oh! We didn't choose it," was the reply. "Father was on his way up north. We had a bullock cart. The bullocks took ill and died right here, so here we had to stay."

He laughed. "It was pretty rough going, too, for a while, let me tell you. But wasn't it worth it! We'd never have anything like this in England!"

There weren't many old settlers left by then, but one gentleman proudly showed me through his ranch house, the same log home that his brother and he had built before the turn of the century. I stood beside him at the window as he looked down the valley. Somehow I knew he was thinking of days gone by, of the strength of his youth and the excitement and challenge of his life as a young man.

"Aye," he said as he surveyed the valley with its fences and the clusters of trees on the hillside, "many a time I've just stood here and looked as we're looking now. There weren't any trees then. It was all bare hillside. The prairie fires killed the trees. It took roads to stop the fires.

"But if there weren't any trees, there were Indian teepees. From where we're standing I've counted over a hundred of them just down in the valley there. It was quite a sight, I'll tell you, with their camp-fires and horses, and the warriors in their buckskin."

"Weren't you afraid?" I asked.

"No, why should I be?" he replied proudly. "My brother and I had rifles. The Indians never bothered us — and besides, we had the Mounted Police."

The Mounted Police! The story of white settlement in the Canadian West must always be linked to the history of the Mounted Police — the North-West Mounted Police as they were called at first — who, raw recruits as they often were and strangers to the West, displayed a courage and integrity that prevented bloodshed, protected the Indians from cruel and unscrupulous exploiters, and upheld the law.

Chapter Twenty-five

The Mounted Police did more than uphold the law. They brought it to the turbulent Canadian West, known then as the North-West Territories of Canada.

Fort Whoop-Up, the headquarters of the U.S. whisky traders, stood about forty miles north of the American border with what is now the Province of Alberta. There the traders dispensed to the Indians a dreadful concoction of raw whisky, red pepper, chewing tobacco and other ingredients that earned for it the name of firewater. They sold that, and rifles, to the Blackfoot and other warlike tribes whose warriors, inflamed by this awful liquor, took to pillage and murder, even across the border in the United States, attacking lonely settlements.

It was a state of affairs that could not be allowed to continue, and in May 1873 the government of Canada created the North-West Mounted Police.

It was raised hurriedly, and luckily for the eagerness of the recruits, without too many questions being asked, for many of them hardly knew one end of a horse from the other. What a collection of odds and sods they were at first! They came from all walks of life and in all kinds of condition, sharing only a near-total ignorance of Canada's West or the trackless prairie they would have to cross to reach it. They were easterners, mainly from Ontario and Quebec.

But they were knocked into shape, drilled in the fashion of British Army units called Mounted Rifles, until finally, after rejections and resignations, nearly three hundred splendidly fit young men remained.

In July 1874, the red-coat policemen, as they were known to our old friend Mrs. Catherine Hogge, set out on their epic march to the foothills of the Rockies eight hundred miles to the west. En route they would experience extremes of heat and cold for which their clothing would often be inadequate. They would encounter swarms of mosquitoes whose incessant attacks tortured horses and men alike, and hordes of locusts that devoured every blade of grass in sight. Horses would sicken and die, men suffer from dysentery, broken-down supply wagons would have to be abandoned, and at times disaster would face the expedition.

But on they pressed, and in October the contingent guided by Jerry Potts and led by Assistant Commissioner Macleod reached Fort Whoop-Up to find it empty. The whisky traders had been warned of the approaching red coats and had taken to their heels.

Both Macleod and Potts would later become legends. Macleod was a Highland Scot, a lawyer and soldier. Potts was a taciturn half-breed, part Scot, part Indian, a renowned scout and plainsman. They were an unlikely partnership, but Canada and the Mounted Police owe much to these two men who served the force with great distinction. Potts, though only a hired scout and guide, showed great courage and loyalty, and with his uncanny knack for finding his way in strange and sometimes dangerous terrain, he saved his comrades' lives on more than one occasion. Macleod, the diplomat and soldier whose word was his bond, brought peace when there might have been war.

The force's reputation for dogged courage and fair dealing has made its name one of the most famous in the world.

Called the Royal Canadian Mounted Police since 1919, they still police the West, though motorcars and helicopters have replaced the horses. In a country where accidents of all kinds take place on remote roads, it was inevitable that Janet and I would find ourselves involved with them.

One accident in the summer of 1955 first brought me into contact with them. There had been an accident on the road midway between Okotoks and the town of Black Diamond. A vehicle was in the ditch and the driver was badly injured. I was needed at the site.

Ambulances were few and far between in those days and so, grabbing my emergency case, I drove at full speed to the scene. Approaching it some ten miles west of town, I saw a line of cars drawn up by the roadside. Men were standing about. At the head of the line a police car, its lights flashing, had been parked in the middle of the road, and I drove up to it. A constable was using a bullhorn to instruct approaching motorists to draw onto the side of the road, switch off their car engines and put out all cigarettes.

I quickly drew up and walked towards the constable, a man in his early twenties. I needed no explanation of his orders.

It was late afternoon, still blisteringly hot, with hardly a breeze. I could faintly smell the gasoline before I saw the tanker truck lying on its side in the deep roadside ditch, facing away from us.

"It's an old gasoline tanker," explained the constable, "and it's leaking. You can smell it from here. The driver's still in the cab, sir. I don't know his condition, but the fire brigade'll be here soon. I daren't move from here, for it would just take one fool to try to drive past it to have a catastrophe."

Far down the road on the other side of the upturned vehicle there was a similar line-up — a police car parked in the middle of the roadway and a constable halting all traffic.

The two policemen were also communicating between them by means of bullhorns — an apt expression, indeed.

"It's all yours, sir, if you feel you should go. It could blow, you know!"

Well, I knew it could blow, and I was not at all enthusiastic, but reluctantly I set off towards the truck, my thoughts — and none of them happy ones — racing through my mind. Still, if the driver needed medical help, there was no way of avoiding that long walk.

I had completed perhaps twenty yards when there was a bellow on the bullhorn of the group on the other side of the wreck.

"Who the hell is that bloody fool and where does he think he's going?"

"It's Dr. Gibson from Okotoks," replied the constable I had just left, adding in that stentorian roar, "he's going to see what he can do for the driver."

"Well," bellowed the first voice again, apparently assuming that I was some ethereal creature unable to hear a syllable of his trumpeted advice, "this is Dr. Harry Lander of Black Diamond. Tell him to get the hell out of there right now. We've had the glasses on the driver for fifteen minutes. He's dead. Died instantly. There's no point in having two of them dead. Get the hell out."

Dr. Harry Lander was famous for his pungent use of the English language, but seldom in my life have I heard sweeter advice. I retreated whence I had come and waited for the fire brigade. It arrived almost on my heels and dealt with the situation promptly and efficiently.

I had missed my chance to be a hero, but the first martini I shared with Janet that evening seemed to have a special quality to it, and the second was better still!

Chapter Twenty-six

"You'd better check my blood pressure, Doc. I guess it's way up."

Joe Snow sat on the office settee, already rolling up his sleeve expectantly, looking at me as he did so.

"I don't want to hold you up, Doc. I can see you're busy — the waiting room's full. But this headache's been killing me, and I've been having dizzy spells all this past week."

A good-looking man, even at sixty-eight, Snow nevertheless was not the man he'd been a few years before, and he hardly even resembled the handsome, broad-shouldered, lean-hipped cowboy he'd looked as a young man. His wife had proudly shown me a photograph of Joe astride a horse at some country rodeo long ago, and I often thought he epitomized the western horseman, tall in the saddle, flat-bellied and sure of himself.

But his wife had gone five years before and Joe had a lonely life to lead, fending for himself, eating indifferently cooked food and drinking a bit too much. Now he had high blood pressure to contend with, and he had put on more weight than was good for him.

He'd never remarried. "I fell for Madge when I was a kid at school," he'd told me, "and it'll be Madge to the end of my days, Doc." He hid his depression well after her death. His two sons had long since left the farm. Both were doing well, one as an engineer and the other as a geologist "in oil," as they say out West.

Snow wasn't a poor man. He was a successful farmer, the kind of fellow who had known hard work since he'd been a boy. He'd ridden out to care for the cattle in weather that dipped to thirty below, when towels on the clotheslines could be cracked in two like sheets of cardboard, and he had a rather kindly contempt for the young fellows who nowadays drive out to the cattle in trucks. He still farmed his land, seeding it to wheat, barley or alfalfa as it suited him, and he farmed it well. He'd sold all his cattle, so the winters were long and boring now, and to comfort himself he reached for the bottle, though he was no drunkard.

In response to my remonstrations that he should be taking life easier at harvest time, yet finding some other interest in winter, he'd replied that farming was the only thing he knew. He'd be lost without the land, he said, and besides, it was really for the boys that he kept it on.

"Sure as fate, they'll come back to the land," he'd say, and I had always known there wasn't much point in arguing with him.

Until today. Reflectively I loosened the cuff of the sphygmomanometer after checking his blood pressure twice, and on both arms, just to make sure. His blood pressure had risen to dangerous levels, and this explained his headaches and dizziness. Like so many people with hypertension, he felt "just fine, thank you" most of the time. Indeed, sometimes he had queried my diagnosis. But he had essential hypertension, which is the commonest form of high blood pressure. Despite proper treatment, it had risen in recent weeks, and I believed I knew why.

The harvest was almost in and Snow had worked day and night. The previous fall had seen the same thing happen. He'd had headaches which disappeared when the work was done, but he was a year older now, and I was convinced that the combined stresses of hard work and little rest had done him no good.

It was time for frank talk, whether he cared to listen or not.

"Joe, you know this pressure of yours is far too high, don't you?"

"Sure, I know. But Doc, I'm busy. Just gimme the pills and I'll be all right. They've always fixed it."

"They may not this time. You could land in trouble."

"How? What kind of trouble?"

I sighed inwardly. I'd told him before, obviously not forcibly enough to get to him.

"You could have a heart attack. Or you could have a stroke. How much good would you be to anyone then — if you couldn't speak properly or had to drag a leg along, or a useless arm?"

This time my remarks had some effect.

"D'ya really mean that, Doc? I'm really heading into that kind of trouble?"

"Joe, you could be. A third-year medical student could tell you that. If you don't take care of yourself and see to it that you get your blood pressure checked every month or so, and," I added, "take the pills regularly as you've been told to..."

"How do you know I don't take my pills regularly?"

"You've just told me, haven't you?" I grinned.

Then I launched into a dissertation on high blood pressure, telling him how in some cases people don't even know they're hypertensive. He got the full force of my arguments in favour of proper care, ending, since I had his attention at least, with a talk on the benefits of retirement.

He looked at me aghast.

"Are you telling me to retire, Doc? What in hell would I do with myself? Sit and look at the view? You know what I'd do. I'd be in the bar from morning till night. I'd be dead in a year. *Me* retire?"

"What about other interests? Hobbies?"

"Well, I still ride. That's a hobby. And I'm good with machinery. But if I retired, they'd go."

"Joe" — patiently — "you could read books..."

As soon as I said that, I knew I'd lost a listener. Hastily I brought the conversation to an end, but not without emphasizing his need, as a matter of urgency, to consider his future, to stop working so hard and to look for some pleasure in life. "And as for the boys, Joe," I ended, "they're not coming back to the farm and you know that. They worry about you. So why not sell the place, or rent it and take life a bit easier. Even if you didn't retire, your neighbours would love to have your help at harvest time — but you won't have to kill yourself."

My patient didn't say much and took his leave. But dutifully, and surprisingly, he was back within the month. Would I check his blood pressure and renew his prescription for the pills? This done, he said that a married brother who farmed in Saskatchewan spent his winters in the warmth of Arizona, and he'd thought he might accept his sister-in-law's invitation to join them. It was a splendid idea, I told him, and gave him a letter of introduction to the doctor of his choice in the sunny south.

"Come and see me next spring," were my parting words.

His case is far from uncommon — a man growing older, the family gone, developing the almost inevitable ailments of aging with the accompanying physical limitations, and never having taken the time to develop other interests that will make old age at least bearable.

Whoever coined the phrase "the golden years" must surely have made a fortune as an advertising magnate. Too often old age means loneliness, depression, deprivation of affection and loss of the vital interests of years gone by, without their replacement by other, more

124

suitable hobbies. And sometimes it means quiet despair.

Ten per cent of all alcoholics are over the age of sixty and a sizable proportion of them became drinkers late in life. Joe Snow was on his way, but he'd have denied that, just as he, like many other elderly, lonely people, would have denied his depression.

Taken in conjunction with his elevated blood pressure, his lack of a balanced diet or way of life, too little exercise to break the spells of too much work under pressure, the future for Joe Snow looked bleak, indeed.

Many years ago I listened to a lecture on the subject of high blood pressure. Professor Glen's advice is as topical today as it was then. Drug therapy has changed, revolutionized the treatment of high blood pressure, but people remain much the same. They are afraid, and they require reassurance, but only after the doctor has established a proper diagnosis, and that, said the professor, is the doctor's first duty to his patient.

High blood pressure is not a single entity. There are different types of hypertension; some types, for instance, are secondary to other diseases. The diagnosis of essential hypertension, the cause of Snow's problems, is reached by a process of elimination and, having been reached, a great deal of the doctor's efforts should be devoted to helping his patient adjust to the worries and pressures of life. Relief from emotional tension, allaying depression, the banishment of anxiety, support — they all play their part.

I didn't see Joe Snow until the next spring, and when he walked into my office I was pleased. He had lost nearly twenty pounds in weight, and that plethoric flush had gone from his face. His eyes had a sparkle in them for the first time in years, and his whole demeanour had changed.

"Joe," I said, "I'm delighted to see you looking so much better. What a difference!"

"Right," said my patient. "You know, what I really needed was a holiday. That's what my sister-in-law told me."

"Joe," I asked, "what about your blood pressure?"

"Oh! It's way down," he replied. "The doc down there says I should maybe come off the pills altogether."

But he wouldn't enlarge on his treatment. He was too engrossed in the successful advice he'd received in Arizona.

"You know, Doc," he went on, "that sister-in-law of mine is sure some gal. 'Joe,' she said one day, 'you've been on that farm too long.

You can't take it with you,' an' y' know, Doc, she's right! Hell, I've been square-dancing for the first time in years, an' I've taken up golf. *Me! Golf!* But she's right. Y' can't take it with you. So I'm selling the farm — best move I've made in years. Yup. She's sure one smart gal, that. Right, Doc?"

"Right, Joe."

Ah well, you can't win them all. His sister-in-law had driven the point home far more successfully than all my sage advice.

It was some weeks later, with the weather at its best, the mosquitoes gone after the frost and the sun still warm, that I sat in a friend's garden sipping a gin and tonic before supper. The other guest was an elderly Scot. Like our host, he had come to Canada as a child, and like him, he'd gone back to Britain in 1914 as a trooper in a Canadian cavalry regiment. Surviving that awful war, he'd returned to his beloved Canada and he had prospered.

But, he said, we all spend too much of our lives at work and, he admonished, being a doctor in a small town was a particularly arduous way of making a living.

"I should imagine, Doctor," he said, "that in your work there's a lot of responsibility and a good deal of strain — never off duty, a lot of nights out of bed. Now," he said, "you're still a comparatively young man, so you won't mind if I give you a piece of advice? Make enough to live on comfortably, then retire. Don't wait till it's too late. I sure didn't. You've got to take care of yourself. I did. Take me for instance," he went on, sipping his gin and nodding at me, "the day I was eighty-two, I just quit!"

Chapter Twenty-seven

In August 1982, the University of Glasgow, Scotland, and the Royal Society of Medicine, London, sponsored the Ninth International Congress on Hypnosis and Psychosomatic Medicine. When institutions as venerable as those two lend their support and prestige to a gathering of medical hypnotists, there must be something to it all.

'Twas not always thus. My friend and classmate, Dr. Graham Gillan, once wrote a letter (on his own specialty of ophthalmology) to the *Canadian Medical Association Journal*, saying that "today's gospel is sometimes tomorrow's garbage." It is a telling phrase. To paraphrase, "yesterday's garbage is sometimes tomorrow's gospel."

And garbage was often the word for hypnosis thirty or forty years ago, even though world-famous institutions such as the Maudsley Hospital in London, England, were using it experimentally. But generally speaking, hypnosis and psychosomatic medicine weren't until recent years very much respected within the profession.

In the 1940s I had the youthful temerity to send a paper to one of my old professors. It concerned one of his specialties, the cause and treatment of duodenal ulcers. My thesis was entitled "Stress as a Causative Factor in Duodenal Ulcers in Soldiers." The paper was a result of my observations as a regimental medical officer. The response was immediate and indignant. I had written rubbish. Furthermore, it was implied, my patriotism was questionable. The British soldier didn't — or shouldn't — suffer from stress, and the cause of duodenal ulcers was well known. It had nothing to do with worry.

Crushed, I burned my manuscript, but my doubts remained, and with them a new one arose — the suspicion that our profession harbours as many learned blockheads as any other.

Now, I'm not trying to portray myself as a man ahead of his time. Far from it. Like a great many Scots, I have, to use that fine old phrase, "a decent conceit of myself," but there's nothing wrong with that. It could even, you might say, be a sort of confession of humility.

It's just that Dr. Gillan's letter set off a train of thought and memory. It pleased me to think that two elderly doctors, Glasgow men both, could retain a healthy skepticism about their own profession and its achievements. I recalled then how we — and generations of final-year students before and after us — had huddled round the great doors of Bute Hall at the University of Glasgow, prior to examinations. And I read that the opening ceremony of the Congress on Hypnosis would be held in that same hall.

Suddenly, over that waste of seas the poet wrote about, I could sense a distant rattling as some long-departed professors of the faculty of medicine of my old university shifted position in their graves.

The trouble perhaps is that we doctors are (mostly) reasonable men. And rightly so. We want to see proof. We want to know that something works. We want nothing to do with anything that smacks of quackery. And hypnosis has been associated with quackery for two hundred years. The shadow of Franz Anton Mesmer has occluded reason for all that time.

A brilliant physician, Mesmer left Vienna for Paris in 1778. However, he had more than merely a decent conceit of himself. He believed that an occult force impelled him, and that he had great powers of healing, powers usually denied to others of his profession. It wasn't an attitude calculated to endear him to his colleagues. But he must have been a bit of a charlatan, for he made a mystery of his methods. Finally the Academy of Sciences decided to investigate his claims, and he was discredited.

Hypnotism was cast into the abyss of disrepute, and there it stayed for nearly two hundred years. Reasonable men caused that loss to medicine. But, writes George Bernard Shaw, "The man who listens to Reason is lost; Reason enslaves all whose minds are not strong enough to master her."

Among the physicians who persisted in experimenting with "Mesmerism," "animal magnetism," or "hypnotism," as it was later called, were such figures as John Elliotson, the first occupant of the Chair of Medicine at University College Hospital, London; James Braid, an Edinburgh surgeon; Bernheim in France; Freud in Austria, and Dr. Elizabeth Blackwell in the United States. (It is noteworthy that Dr. Blackwell was the first to qualify as a woman physician in the Western world, though she was preceded by one or two women who successfully posed as men.)

The way was not easy for any of them. They had to counter the

128

prejudices of their own profession, let alone the superstitious beliefs of the general public. Eminent though many of those pioneer hypnotists were, they faced ridicule and hostility.

We still don't know what hypnosis is, or how it works. As good a definition as any is that it is a physiological state sometimes resembling sleep, during which the subject experiences an increased willingness to accept suggestion.

I think it was Gogol who said that God got tired when he was designing the Ukrainian (or was it the Scottish?) nose and clapped one on, saying, "It'll have to do."

The definition of hypnosis is very incomplete, but as in Gogol's story, "It'll have to do."

But hypnosis is a fascinating subject. My own introduction to it came about quite accidentally in Britain in the early 1950s. My tutor was a stage hypnotist who for a short while was my patient. Appalled at my skepticism and ignorance of hypnosis, he took the trouble to explain it to me and to convince me of its efficacy. I became a convert and an enthusiast. I realized that hypnosis must serve some purpose in medicine. Cautiously, I began to use it, and I read as much about it as I could. I had a few terrified moments — for instance when a patient went into a deep trance and I had visions of her staying that way forever.

"Where in God's name," I thought, "is my tutor? If this patient doesn't rouse herself, will he leave his theatre in London and come up and get her out of this trance?" There weren't any university courses in hypnosis thirty-odd years ago and I had never seen catalepsy.

I've since learned a lot. I've taught hypnosis at university courses in Canada and overseas. And I'm still learning.

Recently I interviewed an internationally known medical research worker, a pharmacologist, on his specialty. Afterward we talked about some of the amazing developments in medicine over the past decade or so, and he talked about the newly discovered endorphins, drugs secreted by the human brain and having many of the properties of morphine. That would certainly explain how, under hypnosis, pain in some cases can be alleviated. We still don't know how hypnosis works, but perhaps we are close to scentific knowledge of what it is. It may be that before long that definition of hypnosis won't "have to do" after all!

Despite the growing academic acceptance of the use of hypnosis in medicine, there still exists a widespread skepticism among doctors about its employment, efficacy and the ethics of using it at all. I suppose that's natural enough, for hypnosis has been shrouded in mystery for centuries, and suspicion dies hard. At least honest skepticism is better than the ribald hilarity or downright suspicion one used to encounter from colleagues years ago.

The trouble, too, is that hypnosis has often been abused by unscrupulous practitioners, and sometimes it has been subverted to evil purposes. There was, for example, a case in the southern United States at the end of the last century. A man had shot a neighbour and at his trial he pleaded that he had committed murder while under the influence of hypnosis. The hypnotist was known to have had malicious intentions towards the murdered man. So they hanged the hypnotist!

Things like that didn't help to win over public or medical opinion. The trouble is that hypnosis can still be prostituted or used for evil purposes and we doctors should be aware of it. But we shouldn't throw away a very useful medical tool either, for it is an art as old as the hills and one that can sometimes be effective in a whole range of illnesses where other more conservative methods have failed.

The druids of ancient Britain were practitioners. Their chant is said to have put patients (or victims) into deep trances. The patients, it is said, would awake believing that aeons of time had passed. Thus, it is believed, Celtic mysticism and mythology were born. The priest-physicians of ancient Egypt were experts, too, as were the physicians of India long ago.

Before using hypnosis, the doctor of today should establish a rapport with the patient. One of the first essentials is to remind the patient of one's professional ethics, going on to explain the purpose and limitations of medical hypnosis, stressing that in medicine it is not a matter of one person's domination over another, but rather a team effort that can be interrupted or terminated at will by either participant. People fear dominance while undergoing hypnosis, and rightly so. It is essential to work with relaxed and co-operative patients. So physicians usually stress this, and remind their listeners that research has shown how hypnosis is essentially a perfectly normal physiological condition and that it works best with stable, intelligent people.

The hypnotist has to study his or her patient, test for susceptibility, encourage questions and then select a suitable method of induction. There are a whole host of those, some involving a bit of gimmickry. Gimmickry, however innocently used, is not necessary and is associated with stage hypnotism which, in turn, is associated with quackery. Although stage hypnotists do quite well in North America, they are discouraged in Great Britain by Act of Parliament.

Following the Second World War, there had been a number of reported cases of serious mental disorders occurring in people who had voluntarily undergone hypnosis at theatre shows. Then there was a well-publicized court case, which was followed by the British Parliament passing the Hypnotism Act of 1952, regulating the demonstration of hypnotic phenomena for purposes of public entertainment.

In 1953 the British Medical Association appointed a committee to study the whole question of hypnotism in medicine. It published its report in 1955.

Hypnosis, said the committee, had its uses in medicine, especially in cases of psychosomatic illness, but it was thought that it might also have its uses in surgery, dentistry and obstetrics, as an analgesic or anaesthetic. It was, they said, a proper subject for research if carried out along approved lines. After more than a century of neglect and disrepute, hypnosis as a part of the art and practice of medicine had come into its own again. The committee warned, however, that it should be employed only by persons conforming to a recognized code of medical ethics.

That is why gimmickry has no place in medical hypnosis. All that is needed is a comfortable chair, relaxed surroundings with perhaps music being played softly in the background, relative quietness and, for the hypnotist, a smooth tongue. It's amazing how most people, if they're co-operative and really want to achieve results, can simply be talked into a trance. It helps a great deal if the hypnotist is well known to them. This makes hypnosis an ideal field of endeavour for the family doctor.

There are many scientific societies for study and research in hypnosis. The American Board of Medical Hypnosis awards diplomas to successful candidates after examination, and many universities hold courses for interested physicians, psychologists and dentists.

Hypnosis is easily learned, and it will be unfortunate if doctors leave the skill to the many lay hypnotists who have entered the field. As the British Medical Association pointed out in 1955, it should be used with care and only by persons conforming to certain standards.

Chapter Twenty-eight

"Gibson, could I ask you to see a patient?"

"Well, Doctor," I replied as I listened to the speaker at the other end of the line, "that's a bit of a difference! It's usually me who's asking you to see one of my patients!"

It certainly was a change. The caller was a Calgary specialist in internal medicine, and a very good one, a man who, over the years, had earned the confidence of Janet and myself.

He was not what I used to call a Messianic physician. If he didn't know the answer to a problem, he would say so, to both the patient and the referring doctor. He had no illusions about his infallibility and he was not only a caring man, but when dealing with some medical conundrum, a tenacious physician.

"Well," he went on, "it's the kind of case you might find interesting. This man is in his forties, on his way up the ladder of success, the vice-president of an up-and-coming oil company. You know the type — a perfectionist and a going concern. He's a geologist and said to be an expert in his field. As a matter of fact, it was the company president who asked me to see him. I've gone over him very carefully. I've done every test that might help and I can't find one thing wrong. His wife, who's obviously devoted to him, is worried to death, and I've had to tell her I can't find anything to explain his symptoms."

"But why me?" I asked, adding quizzically, "you surely don't expect me to make a diagnosis?"

"That's just it, Gibson. As far as I can see, there isn't a diagnosis. I've also had him gone over by a neurologist, and he can't find a cause for the headaches this chap is having. There's no neurological abnormality. We've come to the conclusion that he must be having tension headaches. After all, his work is high-pressure stuff, and he has tremendous drive. So, with your interest in hypnosis, why don't you see him for me? Tension headaches should respond to hypnotherapy, shouldn't they?''

They often do respond, and I told my colleague I'd be happy to co-operate. In the early 1960s physicians who expressed an interest in hypnosis were often looked upon as dabbling in quackery. However, I had just had published in the august pages of the *Canadian Medical Association Journal* its first-ever article, so I understood, in the use of hypnosis in medical practice. My colleague had read the article and had even discussed it with me.

I was flattered that he should consider my co-operation worthwhile and I agreed to see the patient the next day. Hypnotherapy has one disadvantage for the busy practitioner. At least initially it can be time-consuming, and so I arranged to see my patient late in the afternoon when the office would be empty.

He arrived, accompanied by his wife, a pretty woman and an obviously concerned one. My patient's approach lacked the charm of his wife's greeting. He came straight to the point.

"I don't know why I'm here, Doctor," he said abruptly. "First of all, I don't believe in hypnosis, and secondly, I don't believe it can cure my headaches. But I'll try anything.''

He was a man in his early forties, of middle height, and was well built. He had the look of an athlete and until six months before he'd been a downhill skier. He was the kind of fellow who looked you straight in the eye when he spoke, and I was sure that workers on the oil rigs, a pretty tough lot themselves, would find their match in him.

After a short explanatory talk, I left his wife reading a magazine in the waiting room while I accompanied her husband through to my office.

To my surprise he was an excellent, co-operative subject. Individuals who are aggressively opposed to hypnosis don't make the best patients. They tend to resent the concept that under hypnosis they "give in" to the hypnotist and so, subconsciously, they refuse to co-operate with him. I had rather expected this would be the case with my new patient, but concealing my suspicions, I had proceeded with the session. He responded immediately to my guidance, going into a state of hypnotic relaxation with ease. Eventually, having assured him that his tension headaches would respond to treatment, I brought the session to an end.

"How d'you feel?" I asked, as the geologist slowly opened his eyes and accustomed himself to his surroundings.

"Relaxed, Doctor," he replied. "No doubt about it.''

"What about the headache? You told me you had one when we started."

"I'm afraid I've still got that." He nodded, shook his head, moved his neck about. "You told me I'd find my neck and shoulder muscles would relax. Well they did, but it hasn't helped this head. But it's a start. You've convinced me. When's the next session?"

"In two days. Same time?"

"Fine with me. To be honest, I thought it was a lot of nonsense before I came here. For one thing, there's this question of tension at work. Both of the Calgary specialists talked to me about that. Well, I'm simply not a tense guy. I never lose sleep over problems at work. Never mind, though," he finished, as he donned his coat, "let's keep going."

I saw him four or five times within the course of a fortnight. He was always accompanied by his wife and the sessions became increasingly easy. My patient, increasingly co-operative, soon could put himself into a deep trance at the merest suggestion from me. But the result was always the same. He'd say, "I feel relaxed. I hear what you're saying to me, but my headaches are no better."

In the end, I phoned the specialist who'd referred him to me.

"I'm convinced," I told him, "that this man's headaches are not ordinary tension headaches. He's an excellent subject. I couldn't wish to deal with a more co-operative type. And I know enough about him now to believe him when he says he's never missed a night's sleep over worry. There's something going on," I commented.

My friend listened to me, not interrupting until I had finished.

Then, "Let me think about this," he said. A few days later he phoned me again.

"We've repeated the whole examination," he told me, "and still we can find nothing abnormal. However, we've decided to send him to the Mayo Clinic. Perhaps with their facilities they can come up with something. I appreciate your interest," he said, "and I'll keep in touch."

But I heard from the patient's wife before I heard from my specialist friend. Her letter came from the Mayo Clinic.

"My husband has had a tumour removed from his brain," she wrote, "and is slowly learning to speak again."

He was dead within the year.

Some brain tumours are very malignant, and yet it is surprising how much of the brain can be consumed by cancerous tissues before

134

detectable signs appear. In the twenty years that followed, diagnostic technology made such great strides that doubtless today my patient's headaches would be quickly diagnosed.

But I have always been intrigued by the thought that in this one unusual and tragic case, hypnosis, though useless as treatment, had played some part in diagnosis.

Chapter Twenty-nine

In the last ten or twenty years hypnosis has been put to interesting use in medicine. Eminent physicians have written a host of articles on its use in surgery, anaesthesia, psychiatry and paediatrics, and there are textbooks on its use in some of the specialties.

Some people have even gone a bit overboard. I'm not referring to lay hypnotists who claim to take their disciples back to previous lives. I don't think this kind of thing does the cause of medical hypnotherapy or the clients of such hypnotists much good.

I'm referring to the medical use of hypnosis in the law courts. True, memory recall can be greatly enhanced during hypnosis and clear descriptions of individuals may help to apprehend some wanted person vaguely described prior to hypnosis. But evidence by witnesses questioned under hypnosis, even by skilled psychiatrists, can be a very dicey business. Just who is hypnotizing whom? We really know very little about the subconscious mind, and it's my judgement that we know even less about the mental workings of clever psychopaths. An intelligent lunatic (and they are more common than you might think) can make monkeys out of even skilled interrogators if he has a mind to.

Where a long prison term or even a death sentence hangs over a person, the validity of evidence obtained by hypnosis is, at least in my opinion, pretty questionable.

However, in my more mundane life as a family doctor in Okotoks, medical hypnosis did have its uses. The first essential, just as in dealing with any medical case, is to establish a proper diagnosis. Does the child who suffers from bedwetting or asthma have an emotional or a medical problem that requires specialized investigation? Do an adult's obsessional symptoms cover up a depression that should be assessed by a specialist in psychiatry? The G.P. hypnotist shouldn't rush in where an angel or a psychiatrist might tread very lightly. A latent depression activated by the wrong approach can be devastating.

Once the diagnosis is established, however, there are many conditions that can be greatly helped by the family doctor who is interested and can take the time to use the art of hypnosis. And treatment is all the more likely to be successful if the patient has confidence in the doctor.

The list of conditions that may be helped is long. Stress, or psychosomatic ailments, form a large proportion of such cases, but my principal interest was in obstetrics. I delivered most of "my" babies under hypnosis, training mothers-to-be to use relaxation techniques during their prenatal examinations and at delivery, often delighting to see relaxed women, "awake" yet hypnotized, watch their babies arrive by viewing the event in the overhead mirror in the labour room. What was even more important, the newborn infant's ability to breathe had not been depressed by drugs.

True, I treated the occasional compulsive smoker, "charmed" warts away, sometimes meeting with success and sometimes with failure, but it was only after joining the faculty of medicine at the University of Calgary that I discovered there was far more to hypnotherapy than I had realized, even after years of using it in practice.

I was approached one day be a specialist in charge of one of the university clinics. He wanted to know if hypnosis might lessen the devastating vomiting that often accompanies treatment by chemotherapy.

He was treating patients suffering from Hodgkin's disease, a once fatally progressive disease of the body's lymph glands. Today, thanks to advances in chemotherapy, many cases can be cured. Several patients undergoing treatment for Hodgkin's disease were getting to the stage of refusing continuation of therapy because of the dreadful nausea and vomiting that occurred during and after intravenous treatment. The intravenous was usually a combination of nitrogen mustard, vincristine, procarbazine and prednisone. Tranquilizers, penothizines and other drugs were only minimally helpful against the sometimes devastating after-effects.

We dealt with only three cases, but results were interesting, and my colleague from the division of medicine was convinced that without hypnotherapy all three patients would have refused further treatment. Hypnotherapy seemed to lessen their extreme anxiety, and though in two cases vomiting did occur some hours after the chemotherapy sessions, they completed the prescribed courses.

One woman described how, the moment intravenous therapy was begun, she could sense a dreadful smell filling her whole being. It was this smell, she said, that impelled her to vomit. She had recently come home from a trip to England where she had had a memorable journey down the Thames. Under hypnosis, and just prior to being given chemotherapy, we had her revisualize her river trip. She remembered drifting in her boat under a willow tree that grew on the riverbank. This was used as a trigger. She was instructed to visualize a field of clover beyond the tree. She enjoyed the smell of clover, and it was suggested to her that as she drifted under the tree the smell of clover would become so strong that it overwhelmed any other unpleasant odour.

When she told us that she had just passed under the tree and that the scent of clover was overpowering, the intravenous therapy was begun. During the therapy our patient blissfully inhaled the scent of clover. She did have nausea later in the day, but completed the course of chemotherapy, and eight years later leads an active life.

Our series was small. We didn't publish our results, though we compiled a joint paper. However, even a short series like this can point to the use of hypnosis as an adjunct to conservative therapy in some cases.

And hypnotherapy is a fascinating field for exploration. Who knows what hidden strengths and powers lie, still untapped, within the human mind?

Chapter Thirty

It was a glorious afternoon in early September. A few days before, we had had the first frost of the fall. The leaves on the roadside aspens had changed almost overnight from their summer green to lovely shades of yellow and orange. Clinging to the branches still, their colour against the pale blue of the sky made the pastel purples and grey of the distant mountains all the more beautiful. Driving along the quiet country road was a joy, giving time for reflection and appreciation of the beauty around me.

I had finished the office work early that afternoon and had sallied into the countryside a few miles west of town to visit an elderly farmer confined to bed with acute bronchitis. My friend was improving steadily, and after going over his chest and making sure that his seventy-seven-year-old heart wasn't showing signs of strain, I headed back to Okotoks, content with my lot in life.

On my way I passed Catriona and Mary riding Peanuts and Gray. Like sensible people, they were riding in the wide roadside ditch, away from passing cars and dust. They gave me a leisurely wave as I passed.

We, however, were the only leisurely people around that afternoon. Harvest was in full swing. It had been wonderful weather and there was a bumper crop. The fields of wheat and corn, waist-high, stretched as far as the eye could see, golden in the sunshine, a farmer's dream.

The terrifying prairie hailstorms that can devastate a countryside in minutes had not appeared that year and they would hardly appear now. All the same, no chances must be taken. A sudden snowstorm could flatten the fields for miles around, and snowstorms in September were commonplace. The harvest must be garnered, and fast.

Everyone in Okotoks was interested because everyone was involved, directly or indirectly. A poor harvest meant poor sales of all kinds of goods from clothes to cars and farm equipment. The townspeople watched the skies and listened to the weather reports as anxiously as did people working on the land. So many of us were dependent one way or another on the success of the harvest. Even country doctors, before the days of medical insurance, could have a lean time after a meagre harvest, and I remembered a few bills that had been paid in eggs and chickens during our first years as small-town doctors.

We were all living in more affluent times now, I thought, as I drove into town. The streets, normally bustling with people, were almost deserted. It wasn't that the place had been struck by some deadly plague. Farmers and their families by the dozen were working in the fields, harvesting feverishly. The garages were being kept busy repairing machines that, broken down, had been hauled into town for repair, their owners impatiently urging mechanics to "get a move on."

Harvest time on the prairies is always a frenetic event. Farmers and their families will suffer through almost any discomfort or inconvenience rather than "waste time" by visiting a doctor's office. Every minute counts. Many men work day and night, harvesting during the dark guided by truck headlights.

It's strange how city dwellers picture the farmer's life as an idyllic existence. Sometimes, I used to think, it was an existence and nothing more. And yet, despite the financial uncertainty, the long hours often in the cold of winter and the injuries that can cripple and sometimes kill them, I knew few farmers or ranchers and their wives who would have wanted any other way of life.

The women worked as hard as the men, often out in the fields or cooking for the harvesters. It amused me when, after seeing the farm wives driving tractors or rounding up the cattle on horseback, dressed in blue jeans and jackets like the men, I'd meet them at some function or other dressed elegantly and graciously.

But now they were fighting alongside their menfolk to get the crops in before the snows of the early winter that had been forecast. With temperatures that could dip to thirty-five below for weeks on end, haste was imperative.

So the sun-drenched main street of Okotoks was empty. Just as I reached the centre of town and was about to turn the car past the old Willingdon Hotel and up the Okotoks hill towards home, I looked east along the street towards the old Skye Glen schoolhouse, and I remembered when we'd first seen it years before standing forlornly in a field.

We'd bought it for five hundred dollars and had it hauled into town to be converted into a comfortable, if small office. One of Okotoks's first buildings continued to serve a useful purpose in its old age.

As I looked down the street I noticed a car parked outside our office and I knew someone was waiting for me, so I headed in that direction.

"Looking for me?" I asked.

"Yup. Doc, I've brought you a casualty," said the driver, as a second man sitting in the back seat struggled to open the door and get out.

"Give me a hand, Ted," he said to the driver. "I can't move this goddamn knee."

Slowly the patient struggled out of the car and leaned against it. He was a heavy-set fellow of about my own age. His friend supported him as he limped towards the office door which I had unlocked and was holding open.

His left knee was buckled under him, and though they were both big men, Ted was obviously having trouble managing the patient on his own. Together we got him into the office and lowered him onto the examining table. His knee seemed to be locked into position.

I knew Joe Robbison, but I hadn't attended to him at any time, and I thought he might have been going to some other doctor.

As if reading my thoughts, he said, "I don't have a doctor. I'm never sick. But this knee has me all crippled up. I hope to hell you can fix it so's I can get back on the tractor today!"

"How did it happen, Joe?"

"It's nothing new. I wrenched my knee a year ago and it does this all the time. Locks up on me. I can usually get it loosened up by myself— but not this time. That's why I'm here."

"How long has it been like this, this time?"

"Oh! A couple of hours, I guess."

We managed to get him undressed. His brawny leg muscles tightened up at my slightest attempt to manipulate the knee, but I knew not only what was wrong, but what had to be done.

"Joe," I said, "without X-rays it's going to be difficult to diagnose this — but I think you've got a loose cartilage in your knee joint. It's common enough. And what you'll have to do sooner rather than later is see an orthopaedic surgeon and get this operated on."

"Doc," said Joe despairingly, "I can't do that. I'll see somebody after harvest. Goddammit man, you've got to get me back on that tractor today! Isn't there something you can do now?"

"Well," I replied, "I could admit you to hospital overnight, get the knee X-rayed and try manipulating it under an anaesthetic tomorrow

141

morning. But mind you, it'd be a very temporary thing."

"Doc," said Robbison, "couldn't you give me a shot of something that'd put me out — then work at the goddamn thing and get it loose? You know what it's like this time of year! I've got to work."

His remark about being "put out" had suddenly alerted me to possibilities. Here was a challenge for me. I looked at him. He was in despair.

Suddenly—"Joe," I said, "I'll make a deal with you. I won't give you a shot, but I'll put you out. I'll try to get these muscles of yours relaxed. They'll just go into terrific spasm if you're not out."

"How y' goin' to do that?" asked my patient.

"I'm going to hypnotize you. And under hypnosis you're going to slacken off those muscles and I'll wiggle that knee around until it unlocks. Okay?"

"Okay," agreed my patient, "but I might as well tell you I don't have any goddamn time for black magic. But I'll try it."

"It's not black magic, my friend. It's physiological fact. You let me hypnotize you and when you go to sleep you can dream beautiful dreams while I work on you. You trust me, don't you?"

"Sure, Doc. They say you're okay."

"Well, thank you," I replied, a trifle peevishly, perhaps. You could hardly have called it a glowing recommendation. "And you badly want this knee unlocked?"

"You bet."

"Well, then, you're in the ideal patient category. You've got something wrong and you badly want it to get better! Let's start."

So I gave him my preliminary spiel about the medical uses of hypnosis, telling him of its benefits, and then watched as I led him into a trance and deep relaxation, emphasizing that when I manipulated his knee the surrounding muscles would remain loose and painless.

Still, I eyed that brawny leg askance, but when I lifted it, it was flaccid and easy to manipulate. As I worked, I told him he would have those beautiful dreams I'd promised. With his eyes closed he began to smile and dreamily assured me they were living up to my pledge. I concentrated on my task. Within minutes he had full movement, and I gave him the signal to waken.

When he did, he lowered his leg to the floor, gingerly tested his weight on it, then exclaimed, "By God, Doc, you've done it!"

"Only for a while, Joe," I reminded him. "And next time it might not be so easy to correct. So be a good fellow and let me arrange for you to see an orthopaedic surgeon as soon as the crop's in."

"You're the boss, Doc," said my patient. But he was eyeing me thoughtfully as he said it. "So that's hypnosis?"

"That's right."

"Doc, I've been hypnotized before."

"Why didn't you tell me?"

"I didn't know, that's why. But now I'm sure. Want to hear about it?"

"Yes."

"It was during the war. I was in India with the RAF."

There was nothing unusual about that. Lots of young Canadians, impatient to be in action, had volunteered for the British services and at one time one-third of Bomber Command crews were Canadians.

"We were stationed near Calcutta," he went on, "and some of the guys talked about this famous fakir. He could do wonderful things, they said, so I went to see him — on the quiet," he added significantly. "Well, there he was, sitting by the roadside on a mat. I remember that road and all the dust to this day. It was reddish brown and so was the dust. There was a bullock cart passing us, and an old woman. The man was old, thin as a rail, wearing a turban and not too damn much of anything else, as I recall. The strange thing was the way he talked — like an educated Englishman," he added. "My folks being English, I knew," he said.

"Go on," I asked, when he seemed to hesitate.

"Well, I'll never forget it. We talked for a bit and he asked if I liked flowers. Then he said he could take my spirit back to England and I'd see the most beautiful rose garden I'd ever seen. Well, the road just vanished before my eyes, and I'll tell you, Doc, I saw the most beautiful rose garden I've ever seen in my life, before he brought me back."

"It's an absorbing story, Joe."

"So it was all just a beautiful dream, like you said," continued Robbison. "All just hypnosis. There wasn't any rose garden. All the old bugger did was hypnotize me. That was all!"

"Everything," I said, in tones that varied between being huffy and lofty, "becomes commonplace when explained."

"It was all just hypnosis," repeated my patient. "Beautiful dreams!" Then suddenly he grinned. "Well, don't you say anything to the wife, Doc, but your dreams sure as hell beat his rose garden!"

Chapter Thirty-one

"Mr. Snowden to see you, Doctor," said my secretary, ushering in my last patient of the afternoon.

It was a cold winter day in 1967 with the snow beginning to fall and black clouds gathering ominously in the west, harbingers of the storm that would strike the town within the hour.

Farmers could not do much outdoor work in weather like that, and when Roger Snowden suggested that he would like to have a check-up, I surmised that he had chosen his day well, for the office was not busy. Country people as a rule preferred to stay at home when a heavy snowfall was expected, for the cold could be deadly, the snow as thick in places as a London fog, and the roads impassable — a daunting combination.

Snowden was a serious-minded fellow, forty-eight years old and a bachelor living alone on his farm. His people had been English — rather "proper" English, I had been told — and Roger had inherited their ways. He was very formal. Half the countryside called me Doc as a gesture of friendship, not condescension or undue familiarity, and they likewise preferred the use of their own Christian names. I had grown to like that western outlook, where one man considers himself as good as the next, but Roger Snowden always addressed me formally. I, in turn, always called him Mr. Snowden.

"Doctor," he said, without the handshake that is often a precursor to a conversation. "I should appreciate it if you'd give me a going-over."

He was a trim-looking fellow an inch or two under six feet in height, and on this formal occasion of a visit to the doctor's office he was dressed in grey flannels, cowboy boots, a checked shirt with collar and tie and a Harris tweed jacket. He placed his Stetson carefully on the floor beside him.

"Is there something the matter?" I asked my patient.

"Well, that's the point. There's really nothing that I can put my finger on. I just don't feel very well."

He ate well, he told me; he hadn't lost weight; he slept soundly, had no financial worries and he had never really been ill before. Two years previously, he reminded me, I had dealt with a bruised and bloody big toe, an injury caused by his horse stepping on his foot. He'd had his appendix removed when a boy — and that seemed to be the total extent of his past illnesses. His parents were dead.

So much for his personal history. He looked well, but appearances, especially in the practice of medicine, can be deceptive, indeed, and I decided to give him a thorough examination, not because of any clinical instinct I might have had about him, but because he didn't come near our office from one year's end to the next.

I set about my task, looking, prodding, palpating his abdomen, listening to his heart and chest, testing reflexes, looking into the backs of his eyes, and completing what I deemed to be a reasonably thorough examination.

We had a good laboratory at the hospital in High River and I asked them to carry out routine blood counts, a chest X-ray and a urine analysis.

No abnormality was detected in my examination. Roger Snowden, in my opinion, was as fit as he looked, and when he emerged, dressed, from the examination room, I told him so.

"You seem to be as fit as a fiddle. It will be a day or two before I get the laboratory tests back, but I feel I can reassure you that all is well."

Reassure! There's a word one shouldn't use casually in my work.

But he *was* reassured, he told me as he picked up his Stetson from the floor and formally shook hands. And, he said, he would take things easy for a while.

"A good idea," I agreed, adding, "why not come in again in a couple of weeks, just to be sure."

However, when Snowden returned, he told me he didn't feel any better, and in fact, he had been having a few "spells."

What kind of spells, I wanted to know, for it is one of those nebulous words often used by countrymen to denote passing episodes of weakness, though it has a multitude of meanings.

I did my best to extract one from Roger Snowden's use of the expression. But the description of his "spells" was as vague as the word itself. I was suspicious by now and suggested that we seek a second opinion, naming a specialist in Calgary.

My patient was examined, carefully and at length by my consultant

145

friend, who wrote congratulating me on my perspicacity as a diagnostician and agreeing that Roger Snowden was indeed, as he seemed to be, a fit man. Snowden would come and see me, he wrote, within the week, when I could reassure him that all was well.

It was at that consultation, after I had read the specialist's report with its catalogue of laboratory work done, examinations carried out and its final words of confident reassurance that Roger Snowden said something I have never forgotten.

He was a diffident man, and one I think had been brought up to believe that the knowledge and authority of a doctor is godlike, an opinion shared, of course, by some physicians. He looked at me quietly, then said, "Doctor, I don't care about all those lab tests or about what you or the specialist thinks. You've both done your best and I appreciate it, but I've lived in this body of mine for forty-eight years and for weeks it's been telling me there's something wrong with it."

I had the sense to listen to him. Had he been less self-contained or more emotional, I might have let his remark pass me by, but I said, "I believe you. I don't know what those spells are. They could mean nothing — or something unusual. My one remaining suspicion is that they are due to some unusual problem with your circulation."

I offered to phone a cardiologist in whom I had great trust, both as a doctor and as a caring human being, and Snowden agreed with my idea.

Having heard my story and a repetition of Snowden's remark, the heart specialist agreed to see my patient within a few days, and for the time being I let the matter rest.

Four or five days later, just as I finished my afternoon's work, the phone rang and I found myself talking to the cardiologist.

"I'm admitting this chap, Gibson. His electrocardiograph is normal and so is his exercise tolerance test, and why I'm admitting him I don't quite know. But he's an impressive fellow in a quiet sort of way, so we'll pull out all the stops. He'll be in for a few days."

It was a week before I heard from the cardiologist again, and then, "Hello," said the voice on the telephone, "I've kept Snowden in for the whole week. We've done everything and I simply cannot find a thing. And yet — I'm not happy about him. This morning I asked one of the other men to see him. He went over him carefully, then told me that in his opinion Snowden is suffering from cardiac neurosis."

"Doctor," I replied, "I find it difficult to believe that Snowden is the least bit neurotic about his heart."

"I agree with you," replied my colleague, "but I don't see what else

146

I can do. I can't keep him here forever, and furthermore the bed situation is very tight and I'm being pressured to empty a bed for an urgent case. I think I'll have to tell him he can go home tomorrow. And perhaps you'll keep an eye on him. I'll see him at any time you want me to. I'm just sorry I haven't been more helpful.''

I thanked him. I appreciated his care and thoughtfulness.

A couple of hours passed. Suddenly the phone rang. It was my friend the cardiologist.

''Gibson,'' he said, ''Snowden has dropped dead — half an hour ago. It was a massive heart attack, simply massive. He was standing by his bed and just dropped like a stone! I was in the next room. I was just going in to see him, to tell him he could go home. I was beside him in seconds. We've had the whole emergency team working on him. Nothing more could have been done. It's astounding and very sad. God knows what happens sometimes.''

Indeed so.

In ten or fifteen years there have been great advances in diagnostic techniques and perhaps today something could have been done for him.

But medicine is still an inexact science, and Snowden's body had not lied.

Chapter Thirty-two

I have always admired physicians who become medical missionaries, taking their skills, idealism and compassion to far-off places, often working for a pittance. But Nepal, India or Africa were not for me. I have never had that kind of dedication or courage.

When we emigrated to Canada in 1955, it was enough for me to become a small-town doctor in the foothills of the Rockies. The challenge of looking after the people there was as much as I wanted to take on. The countryside is lonely enough in winter, but the facilities of large hospitals were never all that far away. An isolated ranch might be fifty miles from a hospital. Okotoks was fifteen miles from the nearest small hospital and twenty-five from a large one, and the only hazards were the cold, blizzards and snow-blocked roads. We had telephones, and in a countryside where the pioneering spirit still lives there was always warm and eager help from "neighbours" who might live miles from one another and the person who was sick.

In Canada, however, there are still doctors — and nurses — who have to make lonely decisions far from the facilities of large hospitals. They are the ones who work in medical outposts in Arctic and other isolated communities.

With the tremendous improvements in communication and transportation over the years, however, the need for lonely action gradually grows less. Governments provide plane and helicopter transportation. The vast areas of the north have excellent centralized hospitals. Distance has been compressed and isolation at least partially banished by radio and satellite communication that makes expert advice immediately available to medical outposts such as the mission hospitals. There are fewer of these hospitals nowadays, but some are still there on islands off the coast of British Columbia and in Labrador and Newfoundland. The Medical Mission Service of the United Church of Canada staffs them with volunteers and medical missionaries until incoming, independent doctors express their willingness to set up in practice. If satisfied with the adequacy of the service offered, the Church withdraws from the facility.

Before the turn of the century and for decades after, when physicians were few and far between, volunteer medical men gave years of service to the remote communities and some dedicated their lives to serving them.

One cold January night when the snow was swirling through the valley in Okotoks, I was surprised to get a phone call from a colleague.

"They badly need a couple of doctors up on the Queen Charlotte Islands," he told me. "Their surgeon has been called away and they can't find a replacement at short notice. I've said I'll go. I thought I might persuade you to come. If Janet and you would both come, between the three of us we'd be able to take care of most things that are likely to turn up. What about it?"

Silently I turned my friend's proposal over in my mind. I wasn't overjoyed at the invitation.

"Are you still there?" he asked.

"Oh!" I replied, "I'm still here all right. I'm just drawing breath. This isn't my cup of tea at all. The Queen Charlottes! A hundred miles from anywhere across the open sea! And surgery! What kind of surgery?"

"Only emergency work," was the reply. "Anything we feel we shouldn't tackle we simply send by seaplane to Prince Rupert."

Prince Rupert, a seaport on the northern mainland about a hundred miles away, has a general hospital and specialists. That was some comfort. All the same, I wasn't a surgeon. I was a general practitioner who was capable of dealing with *some* surgical emergencies, but my skills were limited, and I said so.

"Come on," my friend replied. "We'll tackle it between us. And they really need help. I'm pretty sure an acute appendix is about all we'll see — maybe a Caesarean section. And it's only for a few weeks. Why don't you check it out with the medical director of the Mission Service?"

So I did that. Indeed, they were in need of help until their surgeon returned in a few weeks. Yes, certainly we should fly out any case that troubled us.

"Don't worry," the director told me, "we have to rely on volunteers at times like this. There's a physician at the hospital, but we can't function with one man. The strain is far too great. He'll be delighted to have you up there. And another thing," he went on, "people who live there are a pretty rugged lot. Indian or white, they accept life — and they accept tragedy, too. They'll understand. Better to have competent general practitioners with limited surgical skills than no doctors at all!''

Dr. Don Watt, superintendent of the United Church's medical missions, knew what he was talking about. An ordained minister as well as a physician, he has given years of service to the people of the western islands and the Atlantic seaboard. He knows the Charlottes intimately, having practised and lived there, but his cheery ''maybe you'll like it so much you'll stay'' brought me little comfort.

The Queen Charlotte Islands lie south of the Alaskan panhandle, 135 miles north of the roadless, almost uninhabited tip of Vancouver Island. The city of Vancouver, on the Canadian mainland, lies nearly five-hundred miles to the southeast. The group of islands is separated from the Canadian mainland by about a hundred miles of one of the most treacherous stretches of water in the world — the Hecate Strait — ominously named after the goddess of the underworld by an early scholarly explorer.

Together the Queen Charlotte Islands, of which the largest are Graham and Moresby islands, comprise 3970 square miles, roughly the size of Lebanon or half the size of Wales. Its population of native Haida Indians and white settlers still measures in a few thousand, living in the main settlements of Queen Charlotte City (so entitled by a man many decades ahead of his time), the Haida village of Skidegate, the northern town of Masset, and settlements along the coast.

The Haida, who form the majority of islanders overall, are a proud people. Physically, they are unlike the Plains Indians I knew — the Stoney, Bloods, Blackfoot and Sarcee, who tend to be big men. The Haida are smaller people; many of them might be mistaken for Japanese, and when they wear their ceremonial robes, one is reminded of ancient oriental lithographs.

They were greatly feared by other tribes who would flee *en masse* into the forests at the first sight of a flotilla of Haida seagoing war canoes, but their seamanship must have been superb, for they were known to travel as far south as northern California, pillaging and taking slaves. Aptly, they have been called the Vikings of the Pacific. But there is a deeply spiritual side to their nature, and though most of them are peaceful — and successful — fishermen today, they are famous, too, for their carvings in wood and a native slate called argillite.

The local white people are usually loggers or fishermen and the two communities live side by side, in relative harmony.

The first white men to set foot there were Captain Cook and his crew in 1778. It is not altogether correct to say that Cook discovered the islands, for the Haida people, as Will Rogers once said of his own Indian forebears, "were there to meet the boat."

The scenery is surely among the most beautiful in the world. Great forests of evergreen — spruce, pine and cedar — line the beaches, for mile upon mile along lonely shores, covering the steeply rising mountain slopes with unbroken spaces of green until the mountain peaks, almost touching the sky, it seems, become covered by clouds and are lost to view.

In calm weather the waves lap placidly and almost silently onto empty beaches, merging with the land to create reflections of unbroken beauty and peacefulness. At such times the silence is profound and the only movement perhaps the circling of an eagle in the sky far above.

The Charlottes' storms are another matter. Enormous dark grey waves, white-spumed and terrifying in their force, lurch and rage towards the shore, spurred on by howling winds that can bend tall trees before them like saplings swaying in a summer breeze.

We had still to discover all this, but buttressed by Dr. Watt's reassurances, Janet and I packed our bags and prepared to leave the next day to work for a few weeks as medical volunteers on Canada's most westerly land mass.

Chapter Thirty-three

The next day we four adventurers — our colleague and his wife, Janet and myself — flew to Vancouver in the luxury of an Air Canada jet, leaving behind us the sun-drenched snow on the foothills and flying into the grey skies of British Columbia's winter.

Far beneath us, as at five hundred miles an hour we seemed to drift through the sky, the jagged peaks of the Rockies reached skyward, range upon range, mile after mile.

At Vancouver we changed to a smaller, older type of plane, propeller-driven, for the five-hundred-mile flight to Sandspit, the Charlottes' main airport. We learned more about Sandspit from a jocular fellow traveller. The landing strip was just a bit short, we were told, and in stormy weather — like that very day — there was always the chance that the landing could be a "hairy" experience, what with wind, spray and the possibility that the plane might continue on a little bit farther than had been intended. Onto the beach, for instance.

One of the Mounties stationed at High River had heard of our foray and had seemed amused at our preconception of idyllic island serenity. As for the "capital," Queen Charlotte City ... he let his voice trail off, grinned and told my colleague we'd find it all very interesting. He'd been there. He hadn't said any more, but I began to wonder about the wisdom of making Quixotic offers of help.

I eyed our plane for the trip north with some trepidation. There was a good deal of low cloud about and if there was wind as well, it was my suspicion that we were in for a heaving old time, probably in more ways than one.

But in good spirits we boarded the "prop-job" and settled down for the next leg of our journey. As I thought it might, it flew below the clouds, giving us an excellent view of the mainland and the mountains of the Coastal Range to the east. The peaks stood out sharply against the sky, endlessly it seemed, emphasizing how much of British Columbia is uninhabitable.

But the mountains we saw that afternoon were not the sunlit Rockies of Alberta. They reflected the cold greys of the winter sky and the sea. We landed at Comox, on the northeast coast of Vancouver Island, took on more passengers, then headed north and out over Queen Charlotte Sound for the last four hundred miles of the journey to Sandspit.

Our landing was faultless. The weather had cleared, and cheered by the late-afternoon sunshine we disembarked to wait for the bus that would take us to our destination. Part of the way would be by ferry across the narrow body of water that separates Moresby Island, on which we had landed, from Graham Island, where we were headed.

The ferry did not impress me. It consisted of an open barge lashed to the side of a small tug, and vehicles backed onto it so they could drive off at the other end; and it seemed to me there wasn't very much to stop a nervous driver from backing right into the water!

But our bus driver knew what she was doing and we took our place with the half-dozen vehicles making the trip. With one exception they were battered old half-ton trucks. The exception was a new, expensive limousine, the kind of state-of-the-art vehicle that was more in keeping with downtown Vancouver than Queen Charlotte City's gravelled streets. So was its owner. Dressed in immaculately creased blue trousers, collar and tie, spotless shoes and an expensive leather jacket, he might have been an advertisement for travel to Paris. But I soon forgot about him as we began the last leg of our journey.

The choppy sea sparkled blue and white in the sunlight, but it was the sight of the surrounding land that gripped us. In the clear air the mountains were majestic and beautiful, rising steeply from the sea, clothed in green at the lower levels, then purple as they rose towards the diaphanous clouds that wreathed their peaks. So peaceful, so impressive was the scene that we felt a sense of quiet anticipation, of security, as we neared the shore.

As we slowly approached our landing spot, however, I eyed askance the rocky, gravelled incline that led from the beach up to the main road to Queen Charlotte City. It looked suspiciously steep to me and I was glad I was a bus passenger and was not driving my own car.

We began to disembark. The driver of the first truck to go off gunned his engine, and in a shower of pebbles made it up the incline to the road. Another repeated this feat, to be followed by the limousine. Its owner drove off steadily and did well enough for the first thirty feet. But it rains with great frequency on the Charlottes, and so the incline was not only steep but muddy and soft.

The automobile slowed to a crawl, stopped and settled into the morass. Advice was shouted. Wheels spun wildly. Gravel and sand were catapulted towards the watchers on the barge. All to no avail. The car was stuck. Its owner stepped out and stood surveying the situation. Disembarkation ceased.

Help, however, was at hand. A truck was backed down the slope, chains and ropes were attached to the limousine, and a tug-of-war began. The car would not budge. Its anxious owner hovered around it, proffering instructions which were casually ignored. Suddenly, however, the car was sucked out of the bog and then, just as quickly, the shining front bumper sprang into the air like a broken violin string at the height of a cadenza, before falling to the ground. The car's owner, standing watching, struck his forehead, then threw his arms into the air in a gesture of despair that, had he been an actor, would have won him the plaudits usually accorded only an Olivier or a Gielgud.

I had shared a seat on the bus with a Haida woman. "Shared" is a euphemism. She must have weighed nearly three hundred pounds, and to maintain myself in the seat I had to brace one foot on the seat across the aisle from me. She had been watching the rescue operation with great interest. Silent mirth, however, now overwhelmed her and she shook, heaved and rippled so much that I found it simpler to stand as the car, minus its front bumper, was hauled onto the highway and handed over to the care of its grieving owner.

What became of him, or who he was, I never discovered, but like our little quartet, he was obviously new to the islands.

Later in the evening I proposed that we celebrate our arrival over a beer. This was greeted with enthusiasm, and I volunteered to go to the government liquor store.

"Six beers," I ordered when my turn came.

The liquor-store clerk didn't seem to hear me. He kept piling cases of beer on the counter. Then, "That'll be fifteen dollars."

"Fifteen dollars?" I echoed in outrage. "You must be kidding!"

"Beer's the same price here as in Vancouver," I was told. "Six beers — two dollars and fifty cents a case — fifteen dollars."

"Oh!" I cried, enlightened. "But I only wanted six bottles!"

The clerk looked at me as if I had descended from outer space, then began retrieving the cases he had loaded onto the counter.

"Jeez," he said. "Six bottles of beer. Nobody ever asks for six bottles up here! Six beers means six cases on the Charlottes, man!"

I trudged back to our lodgings through the rain and the mud. Wreaths of mist were quietly sweeping down the mountainside. Wraithlike, the disembodied tops of trees towered far above me, and I wondered what the next few weeks had in store for us.

When I think about it, I wonder what those beers would cost me today!

Chapter Thirty-four

We had a short meeting with the surgeon before he left. He and his colleague, neither of them young, were successful doctors who had given up prosperous practices in order to look after their native fellow Canadians for two years. Their families were with them, and the year before, one of them, in bad weather and with his surgeon-colleague off the island for two days, had had to give his daughter an anaesthetic while a strange surgeon, visiting on a fishing trip, had removed her appendix. That was a courageous thing for a father to do.

Hearing that story, I was led to ask about the weather. After all, this was January. What about winter storms, I wanted to know? Could they isolate the Charlottes? Were planes sometimes grounded? Might it be impossible to send patients to the mainland for treatment?

Yes, I was told, these things sometimes happened. And what about the large logging community at Tasu on Moresby Island? Who was responsible for illness and casualties there? We were? Oh! So we get there by seaplane? Yes, but any casualties would probably be flown directly to the hospital, I was told.

Logging is by no means a risk-free occupation. Huge falling trees can rebound with tremendous speed and force and even nimble loggers can be caught off-guard and injured, even killed. What then? What if a logger was brought to our hospital with something awful like a ruptured spleen, I wanted to know, and the weather was so bad we couldn't evacuate him to Prince Rupert?

"You'd do your best," was the reply. "If necessary, you'd have a nurse hold the surgical textbook open at the appropriate page and you'd proceed from there. It's been done before," said the surgeon grimly as he closed his suitcase, shook hands, and headed for the waiting seaplane.

I immediately envisaged a steady stream of gravely injured lumberjacks arriving at the hospital, itself often isolated from the mainland by storms, and steeled myself for the coming ordeal.

Strangely enough, this didn't happen. The daily hospital ritual, not unlike that of our hospital in Alberta, was interesting but unexciting. High drama passed us by, which was just as well. We dealt with day-to-day emergencies and soon settled into a routine.

It was in the second week that the weather closed in. Our colleague suddenly had to return to Alberta and was lucky to catch the last plane out. Thick banks of fog rolled in from the sea until visibility was reduced to a matter of yards. And then the snow began to fall.

"It's like a London fog in the Arctic," I told Janet when I came back from the hospital one afternoon. I'd hardly said that when the electricity, the sole source of heat in our lodgings, was cut off, probably by a tree falling across a power line miles away.

We were used to the steely cold of the prairies, but this was different. The cold, not nearly as extreme, was damp instead and soon began to seep into our bones. We could have trudged a few hundred yards and sought refuge in the hospital with its auxiliary heating, but we'd have been soaked before we got there. As time passed I almost regretted not having made the attempt.

There we were, a couple of middle-aged doctors looking at each other in the semidarkness, wearing all the clothes we had with us, including our overcoats, in an effort to keep warm. The silence was profound.

And still we became colder. The great doctor, Samuel Johnson, once commented that a man's imminent hanging must greatly sharpen his wits. The prospect of freezing sharpened mine.

I pointed to the bed.

"Let's get into bed," I said, "as we are."

Some time passed and we began to feel warm enough for me to remark, "Janet, getting into bed with you has always been one of my major pleasures — but not with my hat and coat on!"

Then suddenly the lights came on, the heater roared into action, and we were rescued.

Days passed. No planes arrived or departed and the fishing boats lay moored in the dark, somnolent water of the wharves.

And still no stream of casualties appeared to disturb my increasing calm. Now we had time to gather impressions of our surroundings. We were a thousand miles from the prairies. And Queen Charlotte City, despite the great beauty of its surroundings, was no holiday resort. It was a small settlement clinging to existence at the edge of the great rain forest, most of its residents loggers or fishermen.

But there were others, some of whom no doubt had retreated from the reality of a hard world to seek an idyllic life in this quiet, secluded place. And when they did not find it here, some turned to other means of securing it. "Recreational drugs" were not hard to find, and if their users sometimes lapsed into states of schizophrenic serenity, who was to care — except perhaps the Mounted Police.

During the remainder of our stay, my only challenge was to deliver a girl of her first baby. She was a splendid patient, cheering me as much as I tried to cheer her. Her mother, a Haida lady, refused to leave the hospital corridor, despite my entreaties that she stay overnight with nearby friends.

"I stay here," was all she would say, and that was that.

It was a long labour, and I could not understand why the baby seemed so reluctant to arrive. During that long night I kept visiting my patient and eventually said to Janet, "If this baby's head doesn't descend soon, we'll have to consider a Caesarean section."

Not for the first time, Janet came to my rescue. "If there's no obvious abnormality," she reasoned, "the girl may just be more tense than you think. Why not hypnotize her and get her relaxed. See what happens. You hypnotize patients all the time in Alberta."

Her advice was taken. My patient relaxed, and soon we had a new resident for the Queen Charlottes.

The girl's husband sat silently beside his mother-in-law in the corridor and greeted my news with impassive courtesy. But a few days later, on the morning of our departure for Vancouver and home, the same lady who had determinedly spent so many hours in the hospital corridor asked to see me.

She thrust into my hands a large handmade Japanese glass fishing float. It had probably taken thirty or forty years to drift across the Pacific Ocean with the Japanese current that warms the Charlottes. Such floats, which bear the engraved trademark of the maker, have become scarce and are valuable to collectors.

"Here," she said, "you take. I like the way you look after my kid."

I would not trust it to the baggage handlers at the airport. I carried it back to Alberta. Janet and I felt highly honoured by the Indian's gesture, and the float is still in our home — a treasure to enjoy and to remind us of a very special experience.

Darkness was beginning when we left the Charlottes and it was complete when we approached Vancouver. The carpet of lights, twinkling through the black night thousands of feet beneath us, seemed to welcome us back from our short sojourn as "frontier doctors."

It was an experience we would not have missed for the world. We both knew we would be back some time, but we were glad to revert to being small-town doctors in the foothills. That was isolation enough for me, and only increased my admiration for colleagues who could leave comfort and affluence behind them to care for their fellow men.

A few weeks passed and I was ensconced in my comfortable office chair when a patient of mine, George Andrius, walked in. He had sat around, he said, until the waiting room was empty. He didn't need my professional help. He'd just come to "visit," for he'd heard that Janet and I had been up on the Charlottes.

"Doing good works, Doc, were you?" George concluded.

"Well, we helped out for a bit, that's all," I replied.

"You'd be working out of the hospital at Queen Charlotte City?"

"That's right, George. You ever been there?"

"Hell, yes. I had my appendix out in that very hospital," replied George. "And I'll tell you something," he went on, "they were real good to me, but by jeez they scared the hell out of me at first."

It surprised me that that warm little hospital could have that effect on anyone, and smiling, I said so.

"Oh, they didn't mean to," my friend went on. "You see, I was working as a deckhand on one of those big fishing boats when I got this awful bellyache, so the skipper decided to put in at the Charlottes and get me to hospital. I guess it was early morning when we got in, and the doctor saw me right away. He said I'd an appendix all right, but because I still had food in my belly it would be safer to operate first thing in the morning."

"That all sounds very proper, George," I commented.

"Oh, sure," said George, "and I couldn't have cared less by that time anyway, but in the morning there I am lying on the trolley waiting to be taken into the operating room when I see the doctor — the same guy that'd seen me earlier on. He had some nurses with him and I could hear him praying for the Lord to take care of the patients, and I thought, jeez, Andrius, if this guy has to pray for you, you must be in one hell of a bad way!"

"George," I laughed, "it's a missionary hospital and some of the doctors hold morning services."

"Yah! I know that now," said George, "but nobody'd told me it then.

So how in hell was I to know? I was about scared out of my skin, Doc."

"Yes, George," I replied, "I can see it must have seemed a bit strange."

"Bit strange, Doc? That was just the beginning. The orderly began to wheel me down the corridor, and just as I was passing, they began to sing a hymn. It was the hymn that darn near finished me off."

"George, there's surely nothing wrong with singing a hymn in the morning?"

"It wasn't singin' the hymn that bothered me, Doc. It was the hymn — 'Nearer My God to Thee' !"

Chapter Thirty-five

In the 1960s, when Catriona and Mary were at university, Janet and I decided to attend a course in medicine in New York City.

We knew the American West, but little of New York. Most Albertans going on holiday headed for the states just south of the border — Montana, Wyoming, Idaho — for at that time there was no direct road through the mountains to Vancouver. It was necessary to make a detour into the U.S. for part of the way anyway, so many Albertans elected to spend their holidays in quiet lakeside resort towns there rather than drive to the coast.

I have often thought that western Canadians have more in common with western Americans than they have with their own fellow countrymen in the East. Western farmers and ranchers, especially, seem to share common characteristics. They dress alike, share the same problems and talk the same language in more ways than one.

After all, many of the original settlers in the Canadian West were Americans. They trundled northward a hundred years ago in convoys of Conestoga wagons, the covered wagons of western legend. Their Canadian counterparts travelled west by railroad to Winnipeg, then a frontier town of a few thousand people. At Winnipeg the railroad ended and Canadian settlers continued on their way westward across the open prairie by Red River carts or bullock wagons. It is little wonder that people of the western provinces and the western states have more of a fraternal relationship than merely a diplomatic one.

But New York! That is another world! In 1954, Janet, Catriona and I, as visitors to America, had stood on the deck of the S.S. *United States* waiting to see the skyline of this great city rise above the horizon. Our steward had told us we must not miss the sight.

We were not disappointed. The sun was rising far behind us in the east as with a group of fellow travellers we waited on the upper deck, shivering a little in the cold morning air. There was a hint of scarlet in the sky and then the reds and golds of dawn spread across the heavens, tinting the feathery clouds far above. The sea, a smooth dark grey, like oiled steel, began to reflect the rays of the rising sun, picking up the reds, blues and golds of the dawn sky. It became warmer. We no longer huddled in the shelter of the deckhouse but stood at the rail, our eyes fixed on the horizon. Suddenly someone shouted, "There's something now!"

Pink in the dawn light, the tallest skyscrapers, far away still, seemed to rise out of the sea, growing in height, their numbers multiplying as the great ship slipped closer to shore. It was an unforgettable sight.

Once we landed, however, and our taxi took us through grubby side streets strewn with paper, with garbage cans overflowing on the sidewalks — that was another matter. But the initial impression of vitality implied by that morning skyline never left us.

We were merely passing through in 1954, on our way to visit my wartime friend, Bill Hunt, then a lieutenant-colonel serving in Washington, D.C. Now, however, on our first real visit to New York, we intended not just to learn something of medicine but to explore the city.

We had been well warned of its wickedness. We must not go out at night alone. It was a heartless place. Drop unconscious on the sidewalk and passersby would step around you, we were told.

Perhaps it was St. Patrick's Day that made all the difference. We arrived the day before the great parade. The leprechauns and all the other "little people" must have been working their magic, turning New Yorkers into Irishmen just for the time we were there, because we had a wonderful time.

We had travelled to New York with Daphne and Bill, another Alberta couple, and by all the saints, bless me, they were Irish, both of them.

Sitting in corner cafes having coffee and listening to all the banter between waitresses and their obviously steady customers (all of them wearing green apparel in some form or another) we came to the conclusion that New York is in fact a collection of Irish villages that have coalesced into this enormous city. People seemed to live, or at least to work, in tightly knit areas and to know one another. There is none of the silence or muted conversation that one associates with London restaurants of the same sort.

At night, defying the warnings I'd received about being mugged, I strolled into a bar and might have stepped into a scene from "All in the Family." I wish now that I had taken a tape recorder with me, for what uncut gems of repartee flew around that bar! I came to the conclusion that London and New York working-class people share an ability to see through the façade of pomposity and demolish it with devastating aim.

With the dawn the following morning came the very audible preparations for New York City's Parade of the Year. For a moment when I awoke, I thought I must be back in Scotland, for from somewhere far below us I could hear the sounds of the pipe and drums. But of course! It was the Irish pipes I was listening to! They have a sweeter, a more plaintive note than their Scottish counterparts whose notes, shrill and arrogant, betray them for the war pipes that they are. The Irish being as contrary as they are, however, this pipe band was playing "Scotland the Brave."

Janet and I were soon up and about. It was too important a day to miss. We had a quick breakfast before sallying into the streets where I have never seen so many Irishmen in all my life. There were tall Irishmen and small ones, thin ones and fat ones. There were black Irishmen, yellow Irishmen, coffee-coloured ones and white ones. In the hotel's restaurant while we were having our breakfast, a Scots-Irish piper clad in a Clan MacKenzie kilt and wearing a Scotch Harris tweed jacket, marched in playing "The Barren Rock of Aden" with a fervour and vehemence that could have roused long-departed Scots-Irish New Yorkers from their graves.

But it was in a side street as we strolled about that Janet drew my attention to a company of small boys in the uniforms of U.S. Navy sea cadets. They were rehearsing their marching drill and it was impeccable. Their uniforms were spotless. And the cadets were black, all of them.

The parade began. New York was on holiday. The sidewalks were crammed with spectators. Janet and Daphne stood beside us at the back of the crowd. It was difficult to see past the people in front and the two ladies are not tall.

When Daphne, with her own Irish lilt, said to the person standing next to her, "Ah! Sure 'tis a shame to come all the way from Dublin and not see the parade at all," the information was immediately and stentoriously communicated to the crowd around her. The crowd, like the Red Sea, parted on command, and our wives were magically spirited to the very front, and a curbside view. Bill and I weren't quick enough in claiming kinship, so for the duration of the parade we craned our necks from the obscurity of the back row. The streamers began to flutter down from the skyscraper behind us and the first dignitaries appeared.

I don't know why Irishmen (the southern as well as the northern variety) insist on wearing bowler hats to parades. They never wear them at any other time as far as I know, but watch any Irish parade and you'll see bowlers (or derbies, as they are known in America). Bowler hats, of course, are worn as a matter of course in the City of London by the thousands of umbrella-carrying, pinstripe-suited ex-colonels of Guards and Gurkhas who work there — but Irishmen? — and in New York?

The Bowler Hat Brigade passed, then came the rest, mile after mile of waving, cheering crowds, walking, or marching in a sketchy semblance of order. The New York police detachment, hundreds of them in a body, were given a special cheer. Now, New York being Irish to a man that day, that cheer for the forces of law and order could have been ironic, but there was nothing ironic about the uproar that erupted when New York's famous Fighting Irish Regiment stepped by.

There were pipe bands by the dozen, most of them wearing the green kilts of Ireland. But there were the multicoloured tartan kilts of their Scottish cousins as well, for they were there, too — Irish for the day, of course, and all marching under the showers of ticker tape.

Ah! Sure and 'twas a grand sight!

Chapter Thirty-six

When the next day dawned, it was back to work. But once the lectures were over, we set out to explore the city. On the recommendation of the hotel's desk clerk, we hired an elderly man who owned a Volkswagen van that seated up to eight passengers.

It was a happy choice. We were joined by three other "explorers." They were an interesting trio, two of whom, we guessed, were in their middle thirties. They were superbly dressed — even to their matching ties, which were held firmly in place by gold clips. Their attire and the expensive-looking attaché cases they were carrying left no doubt that they were business or professional men.

However, it was obvious that they stood in great awe of their third travelling companion, speaking to him only when spoken to. He intrigued us. I put him at about sixty, and he was of medium height, grey-haired, blue-eyed, and as lean as a whip. He wore a Stetson, a checked shirt with a string tie fastened at the neck by a piece of coloured, carved desert stone, western riding boots and trousers, and had the craggy weatherbeaten kind of face I have always associated with cattlemen. And that is what he had been for most of his life. Now he was a senator from one of the southern states.

He introduced himself to us in a slow southern drawl, bowing politely to Janet and doffing his hat as he addressed her.

"Ma'am," he asked, "would it inconvenience yew-all if Ah sat in this seat behind you? Ah heah from your accent that yew people are not Amahrikns. I'd like to be acquainted with yew."

"That's right," replied Janet, delighted with this display of old-world courtesy. "We're Canadians, but originally we're Scots."

"Is that so, now," replied our companion. "Well Ah hev a lit' bit of Scotch in me, too, an' a lit' bit of English, an' I guess a lit' bit of Dutch, so Ah guess we should get long jes' fine for the next hour or two. Ah want t'show these heah boys New York. They've nevah been heah befoah.''

Perfunctorily he introduced us to his immaculate and silent companions who looked to me as if they'd never *left* New York.

Speedily we were on first-name terms with our companion. He handed us his visiting card. He was in New York to begin negotiations for a multimillion dollar loan for his state, he told us, and I think the dress, manners and subservience of his two companions annoyed him, for once out of their hearing he described them as ''a coupla goddamn lawyers who've got to be with me to see I sign the right goddamn papers in the right goddamn places — begging your pardon, ma'am,'' to an enchanted Janet. He was no hayseed, and I began to understand why his two companions said so little. He was courtesy itself, but there was something about him that told me he could be formidable.

In a few sentences before we set out, he explained to us how Manhattan Island's rocky infrastructure was immensely strong, making it a very safe foundation for tall buildings. His lecture would have done credit to a geologist and I looked at him afresh. He was not quite the simple cattleman he appeared to be.

The tour set off. Our driver took us first to St. Patrick's Roman Catholic Cathedral on Fifth Avenue, a massive building with its beautiful rose window dominating the interior. Built between 1879 and 1906, it is an adaptation of French Gothic architecture.

As I looked around, I felt that here was a place of worship, that was vigorous, strong and powerful, perhaps reflecting the virility the Christian church once held in Britain. Here in America the great cathedral gave the impression of being vital and sure of itself, like the city around it.

Next we were taken to see the houses of the ''rich and famous.'' Perhaps we were meant to gawk, especially when our guide told us that ''even de bath taps in dare is solid gold.'' But I wanted to see the Bowery, itself once a wealthy area.

''Whaddya want t'see de Bowery for?'' asked our guide. ''All dare is dare is bums. Jes' bums an' more bums.''

He grumbled but he took us. The place lived up to my expectations. I wanted to compare it with the slums I'd known in Glasgow, and those were mean enough in the 1930s, but the Bowery seemed, even in such a brief passage, to be different. Dilapidation was everywhere, and there was an air of menace about the place.

We walked together for a short distance. Every doorway seemed to shelter some derelict, still holding in his grip, in sodden sleep, a bottle.

Suddenly, astounded, I noticed a figure lying at the entrance to an alley. He was wearing a British Warm, a short, heavy, sand-coloured over-coat, commonly worn by British officers of field rank. I left the group for a moment and walked over to him. He was snoring. Stooping, I looked at the epaulets that had once held the insignia of rank. There was no doubt. The puncture marks suggested that the original owner of that coat had been a major.

Could this derelict be the same man? His face, heavily veined, blotched and unshaven, had been handsome. The thinning blond hair matched the straggling remnants of what had been a clipped moustache, and I stood there for a moment, wondering what to do, when angrily our guide shouted to me to rejoin the group who stood waiting for me a dozen yards away.

He scolded me.

"Why d'ya wanna go lookin' at him?" he asked. "He's jes' a bum. Jes' anudder bum. We keep together here. Remember that. Don't you go goofin' off again. You coulda bin mugged an' dragged up that alley the way you waz actin'."

There was one other place he said we should see in the Bowery, though I had already seen enough of it for one day. But he took us to the Bowery's little chapel.

It was an airless place, smelling of unwashed flesh and carbolic acid but, said the guide, the homeless and sometimes the desperate still came there for solace.

We were glad to leave the area and proceed to a more cheerful part of the city. There our guide drew up beside a statue.

"Dis," he declaimed, pointing towards the statue on whose bared head was perched a seagull, "dis is de monument to de late Horace Greeley. His head as you can see has become white wid age. Dat is by de coitesy of de Noo York boids."

He waited for a suitable response, then continued. "Horace Greeley is de guy who said, 'Go west, young man, go west.' Yeah," he con-cluded, "an' de bums is still comin' back."

The senator did not seem to be amused. Steely-blue eyes set in an expressionless face were fixed on the speaker who, oblivious of any displeasure directed at him, drove on, exercising his powers of elocu-tion at every opportunity.

Soon we stopped at another statue, an even more famous one. It shows a beautiful angel, her wings spread, ready to soar to the heavens, leading a soldier on horseback into battle. The soldier is Gen. Ulysses S. Grant, of the armies of the victorious North in the American Civil War, which, after all, is part of very recent history, and man for man ranks as one of the bloodiest conflicts ever. The presence of the angel, of course, confirms the righteousness of the Northern cause, a point that our guide did not intend to be ignored.

He expounded on the beauty and symbolism of this notable piece of sculpture, then paused, perhaps to take breath, or to allow us to admire the work in silence. That, however, was not to be.

The senator had something to say. "Yeah," he commented loudly and deliberately in that southern drawl of his, "Ah see all that. An' if that general had been anythin' but a goddamned Yankee, he'd've got off his hoss an' let the wumman ride."

It seemed to me that the tour ended rather abruptly after that. The senator dismissed his henchmen and took Janet and me for coffee.

I suspected he didn't like northerners very much and that he didn't like having to come to New York to arrange for a loan for his state — just as western Canadians in a similar situation sometimes dislike having to go east to Toronto or Montreal. But then, the world's like that. Northern Irishmen don't like their southern neighbours. The western world doesn't trust the east. And yet we're told we live in a global village.

It was the next week, following our return to Okotoks, that I learned the relative truth of that statement. For years Sunday lunch with our friends, the Willumsens, had been a pleasant weekly occasion and I took the opportunity to tell our friends about our trip. When I began to describe that chapel in the Bowery, an oasis of kindliness and goodwill in such a desert of despair, Mrs. Willumsen began to smile.

"It sounds as if it hasn't changed much," she commented.

Surprised that such a gentle and secure lady should know anything about New York's Bowery, I exclaimed, "You must have visited the place at some time or other?"

"Yes, indeed," said our friend, "I know it very well. You see, when my father was a minister in New York, he sometimes preached in that little chapel. Your description reminds me of it so much."

She said it quite fondly, I thought.

Chapter Thirty-seven

"I'm going to have another baby," said Jessica, contentedly.

"Good for you," I replied, smiling. "When?"

"Oh! Next February."

"That's all right, I won't be going anywhere then. I take it you want me to do the honours again?"

"Certainly, Morris. But you'll be doing them a bit differently this time. I'm having this one at home."

"Jessica," I cried in alarm, "don't kid me. It's not good for my health when you say things like that — even in fun. You're going into hospital like a sensible girl. Of course you are, aren't you?"

"Not on your life," replied my friend, her outward placidity concealing the strength of will which I had long ago discovered was part of her character. "I'm having this baby at home. I have babies very easily, I'll remind you, and I've always wanted to have one at home. This is going to be the one. And furthermore," she added, "you're going to deliver it. You've delivered lots of babies in people's homes. It was part of your job in England. I know. So just book me in for a prolonged house call around February the third. There's a good fellow."

"Jessica!..."

"Don't Jessica me. I mean this. I'm very serious about it. Having a baby is a very natural event and —"

"I won't come."

"That's all right. I'll do it myself," said the lady, who well knew my threat was an empty one. "It's been done before, you know," she added airily.

"Don't do this to me." I appealed to her womanly virtues of compassion and sympathy. "You'll give me a heart attack."

"No, I won't. Your heart is very sound. I've got to go," she added sweetly, ''or dinner will be late,'' and she made for the consulting room door.

''I'm not through with this,'' I warned her. ''I forbid it! You can't do it! I won't co-operate! Why won't you go to hospital anyway, just like everybody else?''

''Because,'' said my very liberated friend, ''I'm not necessarily like everybody else. And besides, I don't like hospitals. I don't like labour rooms, and hospitals are too impersonal. Having a baby is a very personal thing.''

''But Jessica,'' I argued, ''you told me last time that our hospital is better than most. It's not at all impersonal.''

''That's right,'' was the reply, sweetly implacable, ''it *is* better than most, but it's not as personal as my own home, is it?'' And the door closed behind her.

Her smile as she left was no comfort to me.

Jessica and Alastair owned a ranch about twenty miles from Okotoks. They already had four offspring, and Jessica, who loved children, was determined to have more. The pregnancy advanced normally. My pleading was cheerfully rejected. Alastair's supplications, reinforcing my own, fell on deaf ears and my only hope was that in the end she'd relent and go to hospital. I should have known better.

In January there was to be a refresher course in Banff, about a hundred and twenty miles from Okotoks. It was an annual affair, held in one of the Banff hotels that catered to conventions. There would be well over a hundred doctors from Alberta, British Columbia and Saskatchewan in attendance. It would last for about a week, and with lecturers from university centres and the Mayo Clinic, these refresher courses were worth every penny we spent on them.

We faithfully attended the lectures, but we did not stay in the hotel with our colleagues. Our friends, Lars and Hedwig Willumsen, always opened their Banff holiday home for the weekend, and our stay with them during the convention had also become an annual event.

After the daily lectures, Janet and Hedwig would sat by the log fire, talking and knitting, while Lars and I walked through the forest that surrounded their home. Thickly wooded mountains rose steeply on all sides. At that time of year deep snow added beauty to the evergreen trees, bowing their branches gracefully towards the ground. And the snow allowed us to walk silently.

For years Lars and I had been walking companions. We could walk for miles together, hardly speaking, taking in the beauty that lay all around, then as silently share a drink by the fireplace until one of us would say, "Wasn't that a wonderful hike!"

At weekends we had traced the Sheep River from Okotoks, section by section, westward towards its source in the mountains. We had watched deer quietly browsing in the woods or examined the tracks of animals, lynx, deer, coyote and occasionally bear. We seldom saw wild animals. Quiet though we were, we trod on twigs now and then, and hearing two such clumsy beings, the wild creatures that we knew were all around us quietly moved into the deep woods away from us and from danger.

But we were not dangerous. Lars had left Denmark as a young man, and as with so many of us immigrants, love of this new land had made him a dedicated Canadian. He was also a distinguished Canadian. For his services he held not only the Order of Denmark but the Order of Canada. In his busy life in commerce he had found time to serve as one of Denmark's consuls. In his younger days he had put his training as a gymnast to good use as a sponsor of Calgary youth organizations. He had been one of the city's first boy scout leaders and was a founder, and later president, of Calgary's zoo. He was a noted horticulturist, and there were few wild plants he could not name, both in Latin and English. He would be impatient with me who cannot tell the difference between a carnation and a chrysanthemum, but in our walks together he taught me the ways of animals, and I treasure the memory of our Sunday hikes.

The course was almost over when late one morning, as Janet and I sat taking notes on the latest developments in cardiology, a hand was placed on my shoulder.

"There's a phone call for you, Gibson."

I slipped out of the lecture hall to the phone booth that stood near the door, and lifted the receiver.

"Good morning," said a cheerful voice at the other end.

"Jessica! What's going on? Is everything all right?"

"Of course," was the reply. "They couldn't be better. I know I'm two weeks early but I just thought I ought to tell you I'm sure I'm going into labour. Now there's absolutely no need for you to come rushing back here. If there's any doubt about anything I'll send for Dr. Jones. You're simply not to —"

"Jessica. Please go to the hospital. Alastair'll have a heart attack and so'll I. I'll leave for the hospital now if only you'll go."

"What are you two fellows fussing about? This is a perfectly natural event and I know I'll be all right. And I promise I'll send for Dr. Jones if there's any doubt. But I am staying at home. I've always wanted to do this and I could do it myself. After all, women working in the fields in China—"

"The hell with women in China," I shouted, with a fine disregard for much of mankind. "It's one woman in Alberta that concerns me at this moment. I'm coming home."

"I only phoned you because I promised to," Jessica reminded me. "And you know I'll manage perfectly well by my —"

"I'm on my way," I growled. "I'll be there in a couple of hours. And at least let Jones know what's going on."

I rang off.

Dr. Jones was one of my medical neighbours, if you could call living fifteen miles away "neighbourly." We had often consulted one another and I knew he'd help if he was needed.

I breathed easier at that thought and went to the Willumsens' to collect my winter clothing. It was snowing heavily and very cold, and the roads nearer to Calgary were icy, so I was told. I should be at the ranch within three hours.

Lars, however, wasn't so sure.

"You're not making that trip on your own," he said. "We should take two cars. Jock Anderson and I will follow you in my car. That way, if one of us slides his vehicle into the ditch, the other one can keep going. It's safer that way."

We left Janet and Hedwig together. Before I set off, dressed in parka, snowboots and fur hat, I went back to the lecture hall to pay my respects to one of the visiting professors, meeting one of Alberta's leading medical lights en route. We were old friends.

He eyed me in my winter gear.

"Where the hell do you think you're going, Gibson?"

"I'm going to Okotoks to deliver a baby."

"To Okotoks to deliver a baby! My dear fellow," commented my colleague, "I wouldn't drive to Okotoks in this weather to deliver the Queen of bloody England!" Which was saying something, coming as it did from an ex-Royal Navy person.

But our journey was accomplished safely, though it took an hour or more longer than I had hoped.

En route we had to pass Lars's farm. As he turned in at the gate he flashed his headlights on and off in salute and I sped on my way for the last few miles, hoping that disaster had not struck in the meantime.

I hurried into the ranch house without even a pretence of knocking at the door. My emergency kit was kept in my car and I was ready for any eventuality, but I noticed Jones's car standing in the driveway and I took the stairs to Jessica's bedroom two at a time and on the run.

Dr. Jones was in charge. Well — not quite. Jessica was in charge. Let's say that Jones was there. The baby had arrived and only the follow-up work was needed.

My colleague became very formal. He stood back from the bed.

"Please take over, Doctor," he said with professional courtesy, "it's your case."

"Not at all, Doctor," I was very correct. "Please carry on."

"No! No! Now that you are here…"

"I wish," said a voice from the bed, "that you two fellows would make up your mind as to who is going to do what."

We decided that Jones could go home. I was left to do the honours — such as were left for me — just as I'd said I would six months before.

Then Alastair made his appearance, in time to hear his wife issue the cheerful disclaimer, "And I didn't send for Dr. Jones either. Alastair did."

Alastair was carrying a glass of amber-coloured fluid.

"Here you are, dear," he said to Jessica. "This is just to calm your nerves."

"Calm her nerves?" I cried, intercepting the whisky glass in midair as Alastair was about to hand it over — I have never intercepted a foot-ball on a rugby field more neatly — "Look at her! She doesn't need anything to calm her nerves! It's *me* who needs my nerves calmed."

I was merciless. I refused to let her even sip the stuff. I downed it all myself.

"Let the woman suffer!" I cried to Alastair.

"That's a jolly good idea," agreed Jessica's beloved, not without feel-ing, I thought. "My own nerves could do with a bit of help. I think I'll join you."

Alastair, a normally good-natured, imperturbable chap, had been somewhat shaken by the experience.

He raised his glass. "Here's a toast," he said, "to the first — and last — home delivery in this house!"

I got more than a drink out of that home birth. Janet and I became honorary uncle and aunt to the family and I acquired a godson. He's twenty-five now and my friend. He's also the bareback bronc riding cham-pion of New Zealand and I have a photograph of him on my study wall, beside those of Catriona, Janet and Mary. His photograph is quite unmistakable. Despite the difficulties of the situation he's in, he's still aboard a bucking bronc at Calgary's Rodeo Royal!

But joyful though that home birth was — just like so many before it in Great Britain — home deliveries are potentially dangerous occasions. Most home deliveries are uneventful, but some go wrong, and when they do go wrong, despite careful prenatal care, they can do so with catastrophic speed.

I spent ten years doing home deliveries. It was the accepted way to deliver babies in Great Britain until the mid-1960s. My colleagues were highly qualified midwives and I never met a bad one. For nine years, like thousands of other British general practitioners, I was on call to midwives who requested help. The trouble in my day was that doctors and midwives who delivered babies at home weren't clairvoyant — and sometimes they should have been.

In Britain we general practitioner obstetricians could call on the flying squads for support — doctors, nurses and ambulances from the local maternity hospitals — but North America doesn't have that back-up system, and anyone who has seen just one serious, unexpected haemorrhage in a home delivery knows what a terrifying business it can be. It's doubly terrifying when the flying squad is working on a case at the other end of town.

Until a few years ago I thought home deliveries, with all their risks to mothers and babies, were part of history. I'm beginning to feel so much part of history myself that I can comment dispassionately on the ''new'' trend towards joyful, relaxed home deliveries.

Nearly forty years ago Janet and I set up our own ante-natal clinic. We were enthusiastic supporters of Dr. Grantly Dick-Read's methods of natural childbirth and gave instructions on relaxation, but my retrospective view of obstetrics doesn't quite take me back to the dinosaurs.

It does take me back to experiences I'd as soon forget, like the time I answered a midwife's frantic call for help. The mother-to-be had attended a local clinic where she'd been seen by a specialist. An excellent, unsuspecting midwife set out on a routine case, but unfortunately, even specialists can make mistakes, and this one became fatal. The expected normal, head-first delivery did not occur. The baby arrived buttocks-first and the midwife, who had delivered the buttocks, could not deliver the head and shoulders. I found a dead, partially delivered baby and a distraught, shocked mother.

I don't care how well-trained, caring or competent midwives or doctors may be, and I don't care how many hundreds of babies they've safely delivered in homes, there's always the potential for the unexpected.

Home birthing simply isn't safe, even with all our advances in technology. In Scotland, between 1925 and 1930, when home deliveries were the norm, the national maternal mortality rate was a frightful 660 deaths per 100,000 births. By 1978 and the acceptance of hospital deliveries, the death rate had dropped to 9.3 maternal deaths per 100,000 births. In that year only six Scottish mothers died from causes directly related to childbirth.

Alberta, where babies are normally delivered in hospital, has one of the best safety records in the world, and it was a joy for me to practise there and know that mothers and babies were so much safer.

Of course there's the question of personal freedom and I'm all for that. Prospective parents should be educated rather than coerced. They should be fully aware of the risks they take in opting for home delivery. Physicians and midwives shouldn't have to be told, but they should have the right to refuse to co-operate in home deliveries, especially in these litigious times when, if something goes wrong — as it will sooner or later in spite of all the care in the world — promised joy can become black anger.

Mr. Aneurin Bevan, Britain's minister of health from 1945 to 1951, and the initiator of the National Health Service, was no idol of mine. But when he said he'd rather survive in a large, impersonal, competent hospital than expire under loving but incompetent care, he was saying a lot for all of us, and his remarks might well be applied to today's trendy return to home births.

Chapter Thirty-eight

The arrival of the town resuscitator. Now there was an event! It didn't make the headlines in the Calgary *Herald*, and for all I remember maybe not even a mention in the Okotoks *Review*, but it was something Janet and I shall never forget.

For years I had carried a gadget in my car that could pump air through a face mask, and it had proved to be very useful in dealing with a number of emergencies. But the town resuscitator was something else.

It was kept in the firehall. Members of the RCMP detachment and the Okotoks Volunteer Fire Brigade (of which I was an honorary member), and Janet and I were trained in its use, and over the years it saved a few lives that would otherwise have been lost.

It was a fairly heavy piece of apparatus that could pump oxygen under pressure or deliver it in a steady, gentle stream as required. It was maintained with great care and was immediately available to authorized users. That resuscitator was well travelled. It went out to road accidents if needed and it was rushed to homes. Quite a few people survived heart attacks because of the appliance's delivery of life-giving oxygen, the prompt injection of a painkilling drug and the reassurance that accompanied it.

I first met Roland Gissing when he was working on the home he was building just north of town. Although I had never met him, I'd heard of him. Everyone in Alberta who had an interest in art knew about Roland Gissing.

His landscapes of the western plains and mountains were famous. They had been exhibited in the Royal Canadian Academy, the National Gallery of Canada, and were in private collections in many countries. In a unique way they captured the colours of the Alberta seasons and the great vistas of the foothills and mountains.

I was just finishing my day's work when a stranger, dressed like any countryman, walked into the office clutching his right hand wrapped in a blood-soaked towel. His thumb was a ragged, bloody mess, but I could find no sign of involvement of the tendons or tendon sheaths, though they were visible enough, and so I felt it was safe to set about cleaning the laceration prior to suturing it.

"I'll have to do quite a bit of suturing," I told my patient, "and I'll want to use a fair amount of local anaesthetic.

"That's fine. Go ahead."

"By the way, I don't know your name."

"Gissing."

I'd heard that Roland Gissing was moving to the Okotoks area and I looked at this stranger.

"You're not Roland Gissing, the artist, are you?"

"That's right."

"Mr. Gissing," I said, putting down my surgical forceps. "This is your right thumb. You are an eminent artist, and your right thumb is absolutely crucial to you. This is not a job for someone like me. You have too much to lose if something goes wrong. Look. I'll clean this up and bandage it and then I'll phone a proper surgeon in Calgary."

"No you won't," replied Mr. Gissing. "You do it. I've been watching you. They tell me you're safe, so just get on with it, Doctor."

The thumb healed nicely and thereby began a lasting friendship between the Gibsons and the Gissings.

In a sense, too, I became a pupil of Roland Gissing. I painted. Not well, but with enthusiasm.

There is the story of Fritz Kreisler, the famous violinist and composer who, during a concert tour, was tormented day in and day out as he left his Vienna hotel by the hellish screeches that emanated from the fiddle of a curbside violinist. To make matters worse, the man was murdering one of Kreisler's own compositions.

Eventually one day, unable to stand the whining and wailing an instant longer, Kreisler seized the man's violin and shouted, "No! No! No! Not like that! Like this!" and for a few magical moments, beautiful music played by the maestro flowed from that cheap violin in a crowded Vienna street.

The next day as the great man stepped forth from the hotel, the same hideous sounds greeted him — with this difference. Beside the pavement artist stood a large sign bearing the words, Pupil of Kriesler.

In the same sense, you could say I was a pupil of Roland Gissing. He would give me tips, let me read his books, and many a time he asked me to accompany him on his painting trips. But he went far afield and

177

if I strayed too far from town I usually found that Janet had had to cope alone with some unexpected illness or emergency, and there were always plenty of both.

However, Roland trusted my opinion and I remember how he'd phone me and say, "Morris, come up and have a look at a painting. I'm not happy with it."

So up I'd go and while Esther, Roland's wife, and Janet "visited" in one room, he and I would sit silently in his comfortable studio analyzing his latest work.

On one occasion I remember saying suddenly, "Roland — I know what's wrong! It's the clouds. They overbalance the rest of the picture."

Two days later I was summoned to the studio again. It was always a pleasure for me to visit, and a double pleasure this time, for the clouds had rolled by.

It had been one of those times when we could sit together, quietly enjoying one another's company — and I would learn a little more about painting. I learned so much, in fact, that I did an oil of the Okotoks street on which stood our little office. Needless to say, the office was the central theme of the work. The hill to the north, just visible with a bit of imagination, was very, very purple and the sky very, very blue. The shadows — what there were of them — were somewhat askew, but I was proud of my effort, and so put it in an expensive frame and hung it in our waiting room where it was admired by one of my patients.

"Oh!" she cried, "but that's lovely. It must be a Gissing."

I eyed the quiet man sitting in the corner of the waiting room. He, too, was eyeing the picture. And if there was a twinkle of amusement in his eyes, Roland Gissing was too much of a gentleman ever to comment.

"No, Mrs. Peters," I said solemnly, "it's not a Gissing. But perhaps we could call it a Gibsing."

It was a year later, in midwinter, that catastrophe struck. And when it did, as often happened, it was in the early hours of the morning. I was fifteen miles away at the hospital in High River and it was Janet who answered the telephone.

"Oh! Dr. Janet," cried Esther, "could one of you come up — Roland's having a heart attack. Could you come quick?"

In an instant Janet was out of bed and rang the Mounties. Was the patrol car nearby? Could the driver pick up the resuscitator and then Janet? It was an emergency. Then she rang the hospital and left a message for me.

178

Within those few minutes the patrol car had arrived at our house and the constable was ringing the doorbell. Throwing her fur coat over her nightgown, thrusting her feet into snowboots and grabbing her emergency case, Janet ran for the car, and that police car tore up the road as if demons were pursuing it.

Once at the Gissings' house Janet ran in with her emergency bag while the Mountie followed, lugging the town's resuscitator. Esther met her at the door.

"It's too late," she said. "I think he's gone ... he's gone."

Roland was grey, pulseless. The resuscitator team swept into action. While the Mountie delivered the oxygen, Janet began vigorous intermittent pressure on Roland's chest in an effort to get his circulation moving. It was indeed a matter of life and death.

In the meantime I had finished my work at the hospital and was racing back to Okotoks. When I got to the Gissings' house I was greeted by an ecstatic Esther.

"She's done it!" she said. "Roland has just opened his eyes and he's breathing on his own. Janet just wouldn't give up. She just kept going. However bad things looked, she kept going!"

She was still going when I hurried into the bedroom. She was oblivious to everything but her concern for her patient — oblivious to her surroundings, to my arrival, and to the fact that in her desperation to save a life, she had thrown aside her fur coat and was working in her nightdress.

It all remains, etched vividly in my memory — a most dramatic and revealing scene!

Chapter Thirty-nine

That winter passed. Roland recovered and was happily painting again when Alberta's short spring came and went and the long, warm days of summer arrived, bringing with them blue skies, green fields and mosquitoes.

It was a hot summer afternoon, one of those days when even the mosquitoes seemed too docile to bite, and that was saying something for southern Alberta! I was having a leisurely cup of tea in the cafeteria at the High River Hospital. I had gone to the hospital to see a patient who'd been operated on that morning. My postoperative visit over, I was relaxing alone with my cup of tea before me and idle thoughts in my head when the telephone rang. I found myself talking to the corporal of the Okotoks detachment of the RCMP.

"Doctor, could you get to your office as quickly as possible. I don't have all the details but there's been an accident east of town."

"Can you tell me any more, Corporal?"

"All I know, Doctor, is that they're bringing a man in by truck to your office. Your wife is there now and she's asked me to let you know. It looks as if you may be needed down here."

Although we lived in a rural area, industrial accidents weren't all that uncommon. Only a year or so before, two workmen had been overcome by an escape of deadly hydrogen sulphide gas. One man had slumped to the ground unconscious while working, and a workmate rushing to his aid met the same fate. Farm accidents were also a constant and often serious hazard.

I had enjoyed that day's work. It had begun so well. That morning I had been the assistant surgeon at an operation on one of our patients, a young married woman. The surgeon was an expert and I had stood across the operating table from him, watching, assisting and learning. What might have been a malignant tumour turned out to be a simple cyst, and now that our patient had recovered from the effects of the anaesthetic, I was glad to be able to reassure her that she had nothing to worry about. The look on her husband's face as he sat beside her bed had been worth that return trip. It registered relief and tenderness. I was happy to leave them smiling at one another and take myself off to the hospital cafeteria.

I even had plans for a happy conclusion for what was left of the day. I'd saddle Peanuts — or more correctly, I'd con Catriona or Mary into saddling him for me — and I'd take off across the fields with Rough, our collie, at our heels.

And I knew where I'd go. I'd cross the river east of town, letting Peanuts splash his way through the water, shallow by midsummer, and I'd go south across the fields. I might even see Mummy Skunk and her brood again. I'd seen them the week before. Mummy had been too busy concentrating on the business at hand to bother about one amused human being on horseback passing by.

She was trying to get her offspring to cross a fast-flowing stream. She was in front and doing very well. So were two or three of her little convoy, but Wee Geordie, who was far behind and being left to his own resources, was having difficulty. That stream was only a couple of feet wide, but it must have looked like a river to Geordie.

He'd try to breast the water, fail to make headway, then climb out — still on the wrong bank. Inadvertently he'd fall back in and get swept downstream for a few feet until finally, tweetching his protests at all this indignity, he managed to haul himself ashore on the other side. Voicing his indignation and alarm, he was trying to catch up with the rest of the family when gently I pulled on Peanut's reins and continued on our leisurely way.

I was still smiling at the memory of that tiny, soaking, squiggling, wriggling black-and-white procession when I answered the cafeteria phone and found myself talking to the corporal.

"Thanks, Corporal," I said, "I'm on my way."

I didn't linger on that long, straight road between High River and Okotoks and I know I exceeded the speed limit. I took the turn on the 2A highway at speed, raced across the river bridge and into town. The day's business done, the shops were closed and the main street almost devoid of traffic. Outside our office door stood a half-ton truck and a police car. Our patient had arrived before me. The waiting room was empty but for one man, the truck driver, who was nervously walking back and forth.

"They're in there," he said, pointing to the room we used for the minor emergencies that were usually seen.

Janet and an RCMP constable were at work with the town resuscitator. While the policeman adminstered oxygen, Janet was rhythmically exerting pressure on the patient's chest. He was a handsome young fellow, at least six feet in height, and well built, his ruddy complexion contrasting strangely with his stillness as he lay on the emergency table.

"What happened?" I asked, looking down at the inert figure and reaching for my stethoscope.

Janet had looked up as I came into the room but kept on with her work. I made to listen to his heart but she shook her head and said succinctly, "There are no heart sounds."

"But his colour!" I exclaimed. "It's excellent. What happened?"

"He's been electrocuted. He touched an overhead cable while he was working."

She didn't falter in her efforts. The police constable, whose only gesture had been a nod of recognition to me, concentrated on his work with the resuscitator.

I put my stethoscope on the patient's chest. There was not a heart sound to be heard. The man was pulseless, yet his colouring was that of a healthy outdoorsman. I threw off my jacket.

"How long have you been at this, Janet?"

"Fifteen minutes...perhaps twenty."

She was tiring and I took over.

"We'll take it in turns."

"Right."

Janet kept her stethoscope over the young man's heart trying to detect the least sign of action.

"Nothing — not a sound," she said.

We worked in turns, silently and maybe desperately. Janet had already injected adrenalin into his heart. It seemed impossible, unbelievable, that this ruddy-faced, handsome youth was a corpse, gone forever. He looked as if he had simply nodded off into sleep.

"How did it happen?" I asked the Mountie, "and what voltage would there be in that cable?"

"There's several thousand volts in those overhead cables," he replied, "and I don't know how he came to touch it. To tell you the truth, I didn't ask many questions. I just turned the car round, put my lights and the siren on and cleared the road ahead of the truck till we got to your office."

I looked at the young man lying on the emergency table, his blond hair accentuating his youth.

"He's hardly more than a boy," I thought. "He looks as if he'd waken in an instant if I shook him."

I looked at my wife.

"Janet, you know as well as I do that this boy is dead. There's nothing we can do," I said.

"We can keep trying," she replied.

"Yes, I know," I said gently, "and that's what we're going to do. But we both know he was dead the instant he touched that cable. He took a tremendous voltage. That's why his body is still warm."

"We keep going."

"No argument."

The young constable looked at us.

"It's okay with me. I'll stay as long as you feel I can help."

"Thank you, Constable," said my wife. "You've already been a great help."

There were no paramedics in those days, or ambulances equipped with resuscitators and sophisticated cardiac monitors. This boy's only hope — if you could have called it that — lay in whatever resuscitation we could offer in that little emergency room.

We tried. The quiet street reflected the warm sunshine as afternoon turned to evening. Passersby were oblivious to the drama taking place in our office.

At least two hours passed before we gave up, thanked our helper, saw that young man's body, still warm and pink, taken away, then went home.

Catriona and Mary, knowing that an emergency had detained us, had had supper.

Few doctors leave their problems at their offices if they are worrying ones. Inevitably their households become involved. Their children, especially, I believe, are often affected for the rest of their lives by the tensions that arise.

Catriona and Mary, even as little girls, understood far more of what went on than they ever talked about, and later on in their teens they were models of discretion and quiet perceptiveness. They shared the life that Janet and I led as doctors, and to some extent they were moulded by it.

It was Catriona, seeing how sad her mother was that evening, who quietly said to me, "Daddy, I don't suppose you'll want to go riding this evening, so p'raps Mary and I should take the horses?''

By that evening the whole town knew of the tragedy, and later on I tried to comfort my wife.

"Janet," I said, "there was nothing we could have done, right from the beginning. The instant that boy touched that cable he was doomed. His brain was destroyed within a fraction of a second. We both know that."

"Yes," said Janet, who as a young physician had been a casualty doctor in a British hospital. "I knew, of course. But what a cruel fate. He looked so alive, so peacefully asleep that I couldn't accept his death." She looked at me and said, "How fine a line there is between life and death — and oh! — how final."

We are no other than a moving row,
Of Magic Shadow-shapes that come and go,
Round with this Sun — illumined Lantern held,
In midnight by the Master of the Show.

But helpless Pieces of the Game He plays,
Upon this Chequer board of Nights and Days;
Hither and thither moves, and checks, and slays,
And one by one back in the Closet lays.

Chapter Forty

Tradition. There are military units all over the world that have great traditions — traditions that have inspired significant deeds of valour or noble acts of selflessness.

The Royal Canadian Mounted Police, a paramilitary unit, can take its place with any of them, though its tradition is associated in the public's mind, even in faraway countries, not with heroic battle charges, but with stories of the dogged and lonely pursuit of desperate men by intrepid young policemen.

Myth is sometimes confused with reality, but in this case reality needs no legend for support. Serving for a pittance, young constables have protected decent men from evil ones and sometimes evil men from themselves.

My friend, Squadron Leader "Cy" Goodwin, had extensive experience as a flyer and station commander in the Far North. He once told me how he used to fly Christmas mail to isolated RCMP outposts in the Arctic in conjunction with the supply flights to the weather stations in the Arctic islands.

"We couldn't land four-engine planes on that terrain," he said, "so we'd fly over the outpost at one hundred feet in the light of the full moon to make the drop, guided by two flares on the ground. We always took a Christmas tree," he went on, "for those outposts were far north of the treeline. There was nothing but rocks and snow. It would take us over an hour from our base at Resolute, well above the Arctic Circle itself, to reach that post — a collection of four or five houses and a flagpole in the middle of desolation." And there would live a young Mountie; sometimes it might be a married constable with his wife. But that young chap would be the law for hundreds of miles around. And he'd be there for months on end.

It's not so many years ago that horses and the Arctic patrols on dog sleds were abolished. With them, no doubt, went some of the romance associated with the Royal Canadian Mounted, but the police of today maintain the standards of the past.

Mostly.

When I meet, or hear of, a boor or a bully wearing the uniform of the force, I still feel anger, for they disgrace the red serge that is nowadays worn only on special occasions. And I become equally upset when I see a frozen-faced noncommissioned officer change by example two or three fine young constables into faceless, nameless policemen detested and despised by people in some small prairie town.

For the young men that Janet and I worked with in Okotoks for nearly sixteen years were almost always splendid fellows. And some are good friends to this day.

In that first winter of 1955 I was urged not to attempt long-distance house calls on my own if the weather was bad. I should always heed the weather reports and carry survival equipment in my car — a shovel, sleeping bag and a flask of hot tea. A lighted candle, I was told, could keep a man alive if his car was ditched. And, said the police, if I was in any doubt, I should not hesitate to phone the barracks. A constable would always volunteer to come with me, for two men could survive where one might land in trouble.

It was alarming advice for such a greenhorn and I immediately had visions of endless long-distance emergency calls in dreadful weather. In all our years in Okotoks, Janet and I can recall only two occasions in which I needed to take advantage of that offer made years before. On both occasions I was happy to have a husky young Mountie beside me as we drove through heavy snow to patients isolated on farms — in both cases only a few miles from town. But sometimes a journey of just a few miles from town in a really bad snowstorm could be a hazardous experience.

One cold night late in October 1956, we received an urgent call. A car had failed to negotiate a turn in the road between Black Diamond and Okotoks. At high speed it had catapulted across the roadside ditch, demolished a fence and plowed its way into a field, where it had rolled over. Two people were badly injured. An ambulance was on its way from High River, but I was needed at the accident site immediately.

That kind of message was to become all too familiar in the years ahead, and unfortunately for me, my services in similar situations could generally be considered a donation to suffering humanity, for I was seldom paid. It was difficult to keep track of people once they had been moved to hospital, and often the victims were drinkers or transients, who had no intention or means of paying for any medical help.

Constable East was already at work when I arrived and he had pulled a man from the badly crushed car. The passenger, a woman, was semiconscious.

Together we did what we could for them, radioing to Calgary's Holy Cross Hospital that two injured people would shortly be arriving by ambulance. The ambulance jolted its way across the field and soon our patients were aboard. We were just loading the stretcher bearing the woman passenger when, before she lapsed into unconsciousness, she murmured, "The baby, the baby!"

Aghast, Constable East and I looked at one another.

It was dark by now, but East was carrying a powerful flashlight. A few precious minutes were spent searching the ground and bushes around, but not a minute must be lost, and I sent the ambulance on its way.

"We'll bring the baby in the police car," I called to the ambulance driver.

The constable and I began a feverish search. There was no sign of a baby, which could have been thrown many yards by the force and speed of the crash. Our search began to have some of the elements of desperation about it. We were both beginning to feel the cold. Suddenly I began to shiver.

"A baby'll never survive in this," said East. "Even if it isn't injured, it'll die of exposure."

We covered and recovered the ground. Suddenly the young constable looked at the wreck, which after rolling had come to rest, crushed and battered, on its wheels in bushes.

"You don't think it could be under the car?" he exclaimed.

No sooner had he said it than he had crawled under the car and was searching there. Nothing. The mud-covered constable who crawled out bore little resemblance to the immaculate young police officer I had met such a short time before.

Our anxiety had been for nothing. A radio call ascertained that the baby was safe and at home with its grandmother. The accident victims had multiple injuries and fractures, but both survived.

That is more than could be said for a man pinned beneath his half-ton truck on a lonely road one other winter night. When I arrived I found a Mountie sitting on the frozen road, trying to comfort the badly injured driver. He had taken off his parka and had wrapped it around the victim's shoulders in an effort to protect him from the driving wind and the snow. The victim was too far gone to appreciate the kindness or to know what the policeman had done for him.

Chapter Forty-one

One Christmas Eve, late in the afternoon, the phone began an intermittent clamour.

Reluctantly I lifted the receiver. Unless it was one of our friends asking us for a festive drink, I wasn't prepared to be too receptive. Emergencies were another matter.

"Yes?"

"It's the RCMP here, Doc. Could you come over? Straight away?"

"You're kidding!"

I meant it, too. I knew the two constables on duty. Our house had become a second home to them. They played table tennis in the basement, borrowed our horses, and in the course of a couple of years many a time I had been summoned by one or the other of them, usually to road accidents, but sometimes to see prisoners who said they were sick, once to see a burglar who had been shot by his intended victim, and often to patch up injuries received by drunken brawlers.

They were buddies as much as associates. Both were young, in their early twenties, and already they had packed a lifetime of experience into their years in the force. One, I could see, was changing, becoming harder, but I remembered how as an idealistic young constable he'd been posted to the Okotoks detachment and I had watched as I saw that idealism slip away, destroyed by the realities of having to deal with sordid events and brutal people.

But neither of them had lost his sense of humour, and I wasn't too sure that they weren't playing one of their tricks on me now.

"Come on, chaps," I repeated. "It's Christmas Eve. You're having me on!"

"No, we're not," was the reply. "We really need you, Doc — and before the corporal shows up or there'll be hell to pay. Besides, it's one of your own."

"One of my own?" I cried, looking at Janet and the two girls happily talking in the sitting room. "One of my own? What d'you mean?"

"It's another doctor. That's what we mean."

"One of the local doctors, Bill? Somebody I know? Is he in trouble?"

"You could say that. No, he's not from High River or the valley. You lot around here are pretty good. You never let us down. That's why we're asking you to come over. We're doing it because he is a doctor. You could say we owe it. Come on, Doc, just get over here and we'll explain."

What a sight greeted my eyes. The two constables were trying to control a very drunken individual. The floor was strewn with bills of all denominations. One of the officers managed to manoeuvre the man into a chair while the other turned to me.

"This bloody fool," he said, "has tried to bribe us. You know what that'll get him, Doc, don't you? Prison. Doc, will you pick up these bills, count them and stuff them back in his pockets. If we touch one of them we could be in trouble. But it's Christmas Eve, so we'll call it an accident — that the bills fell out of his pocket. And we're doing this for you, Doc. He's one of yours."

I looked at this drunken man, his clothes crumpled and awry, glowering and cursing as he was held in the chair. A doctor — this?

"Yeah. He's a medical doctor from Calgary. We've got his I.D."

"How did you pick him up? On the highway, I suppose?"

"No. As a matter of fact we didn't. We picked him up in a farmer's field. It was kinda funny until he started offering us money to let him go. This farmer phoned in to say there's a guy driving in circles round his wheat field. The driver had got back onto the road once, then come back in again, weaving all over the place. So out we go to investigate. A mile away we could see his headlights in the field, but he got to the gate somehow and we stopped him before he got on the road. Boy! Was he ever loaded! The smell of liquor'd have knocked you over. That was when he told us he was looking for Calgary."

"Calgary?" I laughed. "In the middle of a field west of town, with Vancouver the next stop across the mountains?"

"Oh, that bit was funny. But then he started to get abusive. Look at him, Doc — no overcoat, no gloves, no snowboots, and it's thirty below."

It was unbelievable. Almost certainly the two constables had saved his life, for sooner or later he would have skidded into the ditch on some lonely road, slipped into a drunken stupor, and then, so easily, into frozen oblivion.

The constable pointed to the floor. Ten- and twenty-dollar bills lay all over the place.

"Doc, d'you mind us asking you to pick them up? We're not going to even touch them. And if we charge him with drunken driving, the whole story'll have to come out, and *then* the fat will be in the fire! Attempting to bribe a police officer's a hell of a serious charge."

"What do you intend to do then?" I asked.

It was the harder of these two young men, the constable I'd suspected of losing that youthful idealism, who answered.

"It's Christmas Eve, Doc. I know it's asking a lot, but why don't you and I take him home and forget about it. This could ruin his career."

He waited for an answer.

I didn't know the doctor. I'd heard his name. His looks as he sat there slobbering and cursing didn't endear him to me.

"I'm off duty in twenty minutes," said my friend. "I'll get out of uniform. We'll keep the keys of his car. He can collect them when he's sober and we'll say nothing about it. But we'll have to take him to Calgary in your car, Doc. We sure can't use a police car."

"Bill," I replied, "I'll take a bet you've got a date tonight. And I'm taking Janet and the kids out. It's dark now and the roads are as icy as the devil. This trip will take us a couple of hours — maybe more. I don't know where this character lives."

But even as I grumbled, I knew I'd do it. It was the very least I could do in the face of such a compassionate offer. And all because it was Christmas Eve!

I rang Janet. She listened in growing disbelief, and then suddenly she said, "Go ahead. We'll go on without you." And then she added, "It's the kind of decent thing that boy would do. I just hope it's worth it."

We drove the twenty-five miles to Calgary and delivered the man to his home. His wife opened the door for us and he staggered inside without a word. The door was quickly closed and we drove back to Okotoks, with the car slithering on the patches of black ice. It had taken us over two hours to do the trip.

I dropped Bill off at the barracks.

"Bill," I said, "you once told me you're becoming all policeman, but I think you're a better Christian than I am. That bastard couldn't even spare us a word of thanks. Well, have a happy Christmas. You've earned it. I wonder if that man will ever realize what you did for him tonight."

190

"Oh, sure he will," replied the constable. "He was drunk. And Doc," he added, "it is Christmas Eve — remember?"

It was four or five days before I saw my two young friends again. They were having a coffee together in the Okotoks Koffee Kup. The place was empty and I stopped to say hello.

"Did that fellow come down for his keys?" I asked.

"Yeah. He did."

"I hope he had the graciousness to thank you?"

"Thank us? He was as sober as a judge this time. He demanded his keys, then he raked us up one side and down the other, Doc. He'd have threatened to report us for police brutality if he could. He just stopped short and we didn't dare say a word, or there'd have been hell to pay. I don't think the corporal heard him, but he was in the building. The corporal's a decent guy, but he'd have had to make a report."

"I'm really sorry," I said. "You fellows didn't deserve that."

"That's okay, Doc," replied my Christmas Eve companion, his tone of voice casual, his face as hard as stone. "Don't let it bother you. It won't happen again. Next time, doctor or no doctor, Christmas Eve or no Christmas Eve, I won't be Santa Claus in uniform. I'll throw the bloody book."

I never heard from the doctor either.

But the years passed. My friends are now either senior officers or have retired from the force to seek more lucrative or different opportunies in life.

And then I retired to Vancouver Island, a thousand miles from Okotoks and Calgary.

A few months ago, as I was placidly driving towards Courtenay, our nearest town, an unmarked police car slipped past me and stopped with its red light flashing.

I pulled in to the side of the road. Puzzled, I protested to the constable that I had not been speeding.

"Sir, I never said you had," replied the policeman. "But you weren't wearing your seat belt."

It was a quiet road. There was hardly a car in sight. The weather was lovely. I had been at peace with the world. I had simply forgotten to hitch up my seat belt.

This young man was very courteous, calling me Sir on at least three occasions, but all the same he handed me a ticket for a fine of twenty-five dollars. That rankled.

It is a pity in many ways that the police have to enforce regulations that penalize people for minor infractions of the traffic laws and turn law-abiding citizens, even temporarily, out of sheer annoyance, against their protectors.

I grumbled about that incident all day. Janet was amused.

"You just don't like to be told off," she said with a smile, "and the fact that the policeman was young has nothing to do with it. The road patrol has to do its duty, and you broke the law."

At that I stopped complaining, for I had memories — memories of a terrible accident when in the early hours one morning three young men were crushed to death when their car skidded and rolled over and over. And I remember how the young policeman at the accident site asked me politely if I would use his flashlight for a moment to direct traffic, walked into the deep roadside ditch where I could hear him vomiting, then reappeared at my side, apologizing for inconveniencing me, and carried on with his duties amid the silence of the grave.

And I will always remember that policeman in the depths of winter, kneeling on the road, chittering with cold, his own parka wrapped round a gravely injured man.

They were the road patrol, too.

Chapter Forty-two

"It is baubles that drive men on," said Napoleon in a cynical appraisal of military men and the honours they sought.

Posterity, however, has an equally strong hold on medical men. They attach their names to all kinds of things relative to their trade — newly discovered diseases and so-called medical laws being two instances of this practice.

The passion that can be associated with such variety was drawn forcibly to my attention one day long ago when, as a fourth-year medical student, I attended a demonstration of the names and functions of surgical instruments. The demonstration, usually given by a senior nurse, was being handled on this occasion by the senior lecturer himself.

He was a specialist in surgery, nearing retirement, his grey hair attesting to his long years of university service — years in which, despite his devotion, he had failed to reach the rank of professor. What he lacked in surgical brilliance he perhaps had attained in linguistic acerbity.

There were perhaps half a dozen of us standing around him as he lifted one shining instrument after another from the spotless steel tray that lay in front of him.

"What's this one called?" he'd ask, to which a voice would reply: "Spencer-Wells forceps, sir." Or, "What's this one?" to be answered almost always and immediately by the same voice: "A bowel retractor, sir."

Nodding gravely at each correct answer, he'd replace the instruments. It was a boring business, at least for me.

Suddenly, however, he held aloft an instrument, a small, sharp-pointed thing, and asked, "What's this?"

Certainly, I didn't know, but on such occasions there is always someone who does. The ultraknowledgeable member of our group on this afternoon was the kind of individual who always voices answers about ten seconds before anyone else and with such unctuous celerity that I had come to hate him.

"It is a MacSquirter's penetrator, sir," he cried.

The lecturer stopped and gave the youth a look of such malevolence that my attention was immediately and lastingly rivetted on the scene.

"A MacSquirter's penetrator! D'ye hear that?" he appealed to the group. "A MacSquirter's penetrator my arse. It's a carpenterr's awl," he went on, his Scotch accent growing more apparent in his anger. "Ye can buy them in Woolworths by the dozen at sixpence a time. And what gave MacSquirter the rright tae attach his name tae the dam' thing is beyond me."

And then I remembered the stories of the rivalry between the two men. Apart from the simple joy of seeing my obnoxiously superior fellow student reduced to the level of the commonality around him, I couldn't help feeling that the long-departed Dr. MacSquirter had made a point.

He had given his name to posterity. Generations of Scottish medical students would handle not only the ubiquitous Spencer-Wells forceps, but MacSquirter's penetrators as well. The name would pass into perpetuity... well, maybe not, for someone might popularize and claim for his own a better penetrator, and the name MacSquirter would pass into the mists of antiquity.

If I were to think of something along the same lines for myself, it would be much better to have my name associated, not with a mere surgical instrument, but with a new disease — or better still, with a medical law.

For scientific laws are immutable. My name, untouchable, would go down through the ages. Admittedly in my medical career so far, I seemed to have been most aware of, most affected by, a variant of the universally important Murphy's Law: If anything can go wrong, it will.

Nevertheless, fate will not be denied, and in advancing middle age the opportunity to present the wisdom of my philosophy to posterity was granted to me.

The Strait of Georgia, between the mountainous spine of Vancouver Island and the high peaks of the mainland, boasts some of the most beautiful scenery in the world. And anyone hereabouts will tell you it has the best fishing, too. The locals turn up their noses at mere cod. Salmon's the only truly acceptable fish; and the bigger, the better. And there, on the east coast of Vancouver Island, on a tree-covered cliff overlooking the rocky beach, Janet and I had built a holiday cottage.

I'd just started to fish. I'd fished for a week without getting as much as a bite. My companion was my old friend and neighbour, Dr. John Wade, a Calgary internist and avid fisherman who knows those waters and had fished them for years.

But even his enthusiasm failed to cheer my grumpiness as, fishless as ever, we hauled our boat ashore one evening.

"How'd it go, Doc?" asked Orme Stevenson, owner of the Bates Beach Resort. "Catch anything?"

"Orme," I told him, "there's nothing out there. That water's sterile."

"Don't you believe it," replied Orme as he helped us pull the dinghy ashore. "I'm going to give you a salmon, a nice five-pounder caught this afternoon. Take it to Janet and tell her you caught it."

But Janet took one look at the fish, then at me, scoffed, and said, "Don't try to kid me. Somebody gave you that."

I'd had it. For days we'd been going out at dawn and dusk. I required sleep. Besides, the weatherman had issued a small-craft warning for the next day. I grabbed at the excuse to default.

"Now, Wade," I told my crony, "if you're daft enough to go fishing tomorrow, you're on your own. No more of this dawn patrol stuff for me. And," I added, knowing my friend of old, "don't come for me either. I'll be in bed. Every door and window in our house will be locked."

But at dawn I was gently shaken awake.

"How in the Hades did you get in?" I hissed.

"You forgot to lock the basement door," whispered John. "Get up. It's as calm as a millpond. A beautiful fishing morning."

So I bumbled into my clothes and in the predawn light stumbled down to the beach.

There I made my first mistake of what was to be a momentous day. Whether from sleepiness, grumpiness or eagerness to reach the fishing grounds no longer matters, but I forgot to throw into the dinghy the gaff and the blunt instrument known locally as a salmon bonker.

We'd been fishing for about three hours with our usual success when it became evident that the weatherman hadn't been an alarmist. The sea became decidedly choppy.

We were a mile or so out when the commanding officer decided to head for shore, a decision with which I wholeheartedly agreed. We had young John Wade with us that morning, then a student, now a physician like his father.

The lines were hauled in — all but mine.

"I'll just keep it in the water a big longer," I told the skipper. "I'm sick of catching nothing. I'll have one final try."

About a minute after that something happened to my rod. It began to dance like a mad thing and nearly flew out of my grip.

"John," I cried, "my string must be caught on a log!"

Floating logs, or deadheads, are a constant hazard to boaters and fishermen, but John was not deceived.

Before dealing with this new situation he took the time to admonish me. "That is not a string," he said severely as he stopped the outboard. "It is a rod and line — a ten-pound test line with an attached red, white and blue bucktail lure."

"Well, string or line," I cried, "it's caught on something."

"I'd say it's caught on a very big fish," replied John as he manoeuvred the dinghy.

It was at that point that the salmon broke surface and leapt into the air. It was about fifty yards behind us and the fight was on. My companions and I were astounded at its size.

In retrospect, perhaps we were just a little foolhardy. We were one mile from shore and the waves had become alarmingly high, before — three hours later — we pulled alongside our quarry. It was lying on its side, almost belly-up. The blame for the lack of a gaff, or salmon bonker (in Scotland, it's known as a priest), had previously been apportioned with some acerbity. Obviously, their absence complicated matters, and our net, suitable for landing five-pounders, was woefully inadequate.

Nevertheless, John devised a plan of action. He would put his hand in the salmon's gills. I would put my arm round it and simultaneously we would haul it in while young John balanced the boat.

This stratagem worked like a charm. Despite its great size, we hauled it in. Whereupon it revived, and let me tell you, a frantic fifty-pound fish leaping about in a car-top boat in rough seas does little for the stability of the vessel! However, an acute instinct for self-preservation drove me to doff one of my hiking boots, which made an ideal salmon silencer.

We immediately made for shore, to be greeted by our wives, relief being mingled with disbelief as they saw our catch. I now made my second mistake of the day. I showed it off to all our neighbours before taking it to Orme Stevenson's resort.

The triumph of the occasion was infectious, and it was a procession of relatives and friends that accompanied the salmon to the weigh-in. John, who I do believe would have given an arm and half a leg to have caught the brute himself, was my most enthusiastic supporter.

"Orme," I said, "remember that wee fish I said I might catch? I've brought it to weigh in."

Orme good-humouredly asked me to bring my catch in, raised his eyebrows when I asked for his help, looked in the trunk of the car, called upon the Deity to witness the scene and promptly phoned the radio station.

"It's the biggest tyee that's ever been caught in these waters," he exclaimed as he detailed matters to the radio announcer who asked to speak to me.

"D'you want a free commercial, Orme?" I asked in a hurried aside before I spoke to the announcer. "Yes," I told the chap at the other end of the line, "it weighs in at forty-nine pounds, eleven ounces, and it's three feet ten inches long. Yes, caught off Bates Beach Resort. Bates Beach. That's right. Bates..."

"It would have been three pounds heavier," said Orme afterward, "if you hadn't wasted time taking it round to all your neighbours. Fish get dehydrated, too, you know, Doctor."

However, next day I could have walked on water, as far as Orme was concerned. I wasn't up to that. But I could almost have walked from boat to boat. There seemed to be hundreds of them, all just off Bates Beach Resort.

That same day I became B.C.'s Prince Fisherman of the Year. And I'd have been King, but a week later some bloated plutocrat in a yacht filched my crown by catching a fifty-one pounder off Rivers Inlet.

And so it was that I propounded Gibson's Law of Fishing, which states: If you are there when the fish are there and throw a suitable device over the side, any fool may catch a fish.

Chapter Forty-three

As the years went by our practice grew, but it never really became large enough for us to be able to attract another doctor to practise in the town which, in the ten years we'd been there, had increased its population by only a few hundred people.

And yet we were on call seven days a week, twenty-four hours a day. I have friends who practise in much the same kind of situation, but most of them had the facilities of a small community hospital close by, even if it was a one-man hospital.

Our converted Skye Glen shoolhouse had to serve as our office and the district's emergency room, and many a time it was put to hectic use. I used to feel that we could attract more patients and so support two medical families if we could persuade a younger doctor to join us. It would have meant "building the practice up" for a year or two perhaps, but I'm sure we would have succeeded. However, in the 1960s, it was almost impossible to induce doctors to settle in small country towns such as Okotoks. The first question I was always asked was, "Do you have a hospital in town?" When my answer was a shake of the head, I knew once again that our hopes of finding help were dashed.

A number of factors worked against our aspirations to attract associates. Surprisingly in such a new country, Canadian doctors didn't usually like to practise in small towns. If they were married men, their wives often felt lonely and socially isolated, and sometimes they were unsure of the adequacy of the educational facilities available to their children.

Yet the Okotoks High School has produced men and women who today are doctors, teachers, lawyers, engineers, geologists, officers in Canada's Armed Forces and university professors. Mary and Catriona, after leaving school, went to university, Mary to qualify as a teacher and Catriona to qualify, with distinction, as a lawyer at Queen's University in eastern Canada. Who could ask for better than that from a small town in the foothills of the Rockies?

Our search for help, however, was not entirely hopeless. We did occasionally have doctors work with us for a few months at a time. Usually they were British immigrants who told us frankly that they were "looking around for something," but would work with us until they found the kind of situation they wanted.

It was fair enough, for with a population bordering on eight hundred people and few of them encumbered by this world's riches, Okotoks was in no danger of becoming western Canada's Harley Street. And with Calgary growing rapidly, opportunities abounded to set up busy practices there. Indeed, some of our colleagues and friends in the city told Janet and me that we "needed our heads examined" for staying in Okotoks.

But there is more to life than having the facilities of modern cities close at hand, however attractive they might be. We loved our work in Okotoks. The only disadvantage was that as the years passed and we approached the half-century mark, we realized the going would not get any easier.

Our only relief was to leave the town for an afternoon or a weekend, and when we did, something always seemed to happen. Our colleagues in High River, helpful though they always tried to be, were often over-worked themselves and the city hospitals were miles away.

So when cars collided or turned over in the ditch and no doctor was in town, the Mounted Police did what they could. The volunteer fire brigade was a great help in such emergencies, but once when a friend had a heart attack, Janet and I were attending a lecture in Calgary and no skilled help was available. He died before help finally arrived. We were never offered a word of reproach, but we were mightily relieved when, even for a few months, we had another doctor working with us.

Undoubtedly the most helpful, the most successful and the brightest of them all was a young woman doctor who had come from England, eager to see something of this new land. Janet and she shared the same ideas about the practice of medicine, and they also shared the same sense of humour, which made life easier for them, if not always for me, for not infrequently — medically speaking — they ganged up on me.

After all, I was the titular head of the firm, at least in my opinion, by virtue of age if nothing else, being two weeks older than my wife and heaven alone knows how much older than our young associate.

The variety of cases we saw in that little town over the years still

amazes me when I think back. Sometimes they would be very complicated cases, too. We saw, for instance, a surprising number of brain
tumours. They can mimic so many conditions, especially in their early
stages when diagnosis can be difficult. They can cause what seems to
be simple nervous breakdowns, or a sufferer can seem, even to his own
family, to be needlessly moody all of a sudden and for no good reason.
They can cause insomnia, "migraine headaches," and the signs of mental
breakdown or deterioration of the most bizarre kind. Then diabetes was
surprisingly common, and with so many people of pioneering stock
related to one another by blood and marriage, Okotoks would have been
a paradise for geneticists, if we'd had many — or *any* — around thirty
years ago.

I would see a case that interested and puzzled me, carry out an examination and announce at lunch time that the patient would be admitted
to hospital for further examination that afternoon. The tentative
diagnosis, I would pontificate, was so-and-so.

"That sounds interesting," my two colleagues would chorus, looking at one another. "Why don't *we* go up and have a look?" And off
they'd go together to the hospital at High River, repeat my examination, sometimes do a bit more, then return to the house, where as like
as not I'd come home after my afternoon office session to find the sitting room floor littered with medical textbooks and a discussion in full
swing. I've sometimes had to step over or around books just to get
within earshot of the consultation.

"Morris," they'd say, sometimes in unison, "you're wacky. That's
no more a case of gastroenteropathy of the thingummabobber than my
eye. The child has simple diarrhoea — the trots and nothing more,
chum." Sometimes, too, there'd be a dissenting opinion between them.
And sometimes they'd have to admit that I was right!

This kind of experience made for good medicine. It was competitive
yet co-operative practice, and if ever our patients were well looked after
it was in those happy months. But our young friend decided to specialize,
and returned to England. Several years later she told us how much she
had enjoyed her work in that old converted Skye Glen schoolhouse of
ours and recalled the many surprising and interesting cases she'd seen
there.

But Canada, especially western Canada, is not everyone's cup of tea.
At one point I tried to tempt an old friend and colleague to come and
join us. Wisely, perhaps, he declined my invitation. He would have been
successful. He is an affable and competent practitioner, but sometimes

newcomers are depressed by the change of scene and way of life. Experience taught both Janet and me never to give definitive advice or encouragement about emigration.

One doctor gave notice within two hours of arriving in Okotoks. The town and the countryside appalled him. Perhaps, he said, he should have gone to eastern Canada, where living conditions and customs were more like those of England. Okotoks was like no place he'd ever seen. There was no pub, he complained, where one could relax over a beer as one could in England with people of one's own social class. There was a bar in the Willingdon Hotel, but the law demanded that customers remain seated at tables while drinking. Our colleague found this extraordinary, but there was a reason for it. Not so long ago this had been the frontier, and it's sometimes not a bad idea to have a table between two men having a few drinks together!

I sympathized with this newcomer and told him he'd soon get used to western ways. But he never did. However, he asked if he could stay with us until he made up his mind as to where he wanted to go. He was very conscious of his social position.

"Am I expected to shake hands with every peasant in your bloody village?" he once asked me, and when I replied that a handshake was a western courtesy, he snorted, "Well, I've had enough of it. I stared one fellow down this morning and I shall keep on doing so."

One night we drove back from the hospital together. I was still trying to convince him that beauty lay all around us, and I made a detour, taking him over hilly country to a vantage point where I often stopped.

The only sounds were the gentle sighing of the night breezes passing through the roadside aspens and the distant howling of coyotes. The sky was superb, a deep mauve, with myriads of stars twinkling in the cloudless heavens.

"Let's step outside, Bent, just for a moment," I suggested.

Reluctantly my colleague followed me.

"Look at it!" I appealed to him. "Just look up there and listen."

We stood as still as statues. To the north there swung the great multihued curtain of the northern lights. As we watched, it folded and unfolded constantly. Magically, it seemed to be suspended in the night sky, its colours changing endlessly. We could hear it crackling in the still air. To the east and south the rolling countryside was bathed in reflected light and to the west we could see the mass of the Rockies, reflecting the deep purples and golds of the sky.

"Don't you see beauty in all this — in the Rockies?" I asked.

But his only answer was that the Rockies, as far as he was concerned, were simply great chunks of concrete. I gave up.

Beauty is in the eye of the beholder. My colleague loathed the emptiness of the West and what he felt to be its loneliness.

General practice perhaps was not for him. He would probably have done very well, even brilliantly, as a research worker, for he was academically very bright, and in research one does not always need to deal directly with people.

The trouble was that undue modesty was not part of his make-up, and patients were quickly informed of his high intellectual qualities. The inference — of which his listeners were not unaware — was that these qualities were being wasted in Okotoks.

He stayed for a few months. The West — and perhaps Canada — was not for him. We parted on good terms, and so Janet and I were on our own again. A few days later I was driving along the main street when one of our patients waved me down. He was a rancher, in town to collect the week's groceries. He thrust his head at the open window of my car. He was a bit deaf, so he shouted in normal conversation as so many partially deaf people do. There were quite a few passersby, so you could by no means have called it a private conversation.

"I hear your sidekick's up and gone, Doc," he bellowed.

"That's right, Hank. I think he's going back to the Old Country."

"Too bad," roared my friend. "But I'll tell you something — give you a bit of advice. Doc, next time you get help, don't get some clever bugger. Just get a guy like yourself."

Chapter Forty-four

This is the story of a Stetson hat. I once owned one. It was light beige in colour. I never wore it openly in Okotoks. I wore it in the solitude of the mountains to shield my face from the fierce rays of the sun when I went riding during the summer months.

If I had been riding with my cronies, I doffed the Stetson as we approached Okotoks and laid it on the dashboard of the truck. True, my friend Howard Steele once picked it up and crammed it back on my head, saying, "Wear it, you've earned the right," but I was always too embarrassed to take his advice.

Then I spilt blue dye on it, so, though I continued to wear it on my riding forays, I had ample excuse to discard it once we neared civilization.

Now, good Stetsons are not cheap. They can be costly in fact, so with that Scottish propensity for thrift, I decided I could do quite well with my partly dyed hat. I never owned another, though I bought another, and it is the one I bought years later that I'm writing about.

For a year or two I served on the board of the Calgary and District Medical Society. It was a pleasant chore. The board were a friendly lot and mostly well known to me. Our duties were hardly earth-shaking, however, and board affairs were seldom the cause of irascible debate.

Among our other tasks, we decided on the types and dates of medical lectures to be given that season and we also decided on the social occasions that should be organized. It was in connection with the latter function that I raise the matter of the Stetson.

Each year, in rotation, one of Canada's provinces hosts the annual meeting of the Canadian Medical Association. These are prestigious events, often attracting eminent visitors not only from distant centres in Canada, but from equally important centres in other countries.

It was Calgary's turn to host the meeting, and Western hospitality being renowned, the society intended to make a noteworthy effort to entertain our guests. The issues were debated hotly and at length. It had all but been decided that we would put on a grand barbecue at Calgary's Happy Valley, when in the full flush of Western pride I interrupted the proceeding.

"You can't do that!" I cried. "A barbecue! At Happy Valley! There are barbecues being held at Happy Valleys from Halifax to Vancouver. My dear chaps — this is the Wild West. What we want is a rodeo!"

There was a stunned silence as my colleagues slowly digested this suggestion. Then followed cries of "Come off it, Gibson!" and "How could *we* put on a rodeo?"

But I stuck to my guns.

"I'm deadly serious," I protested, "and it needn't cost much. All we need to do is go down to Okotoks and talk to the boys. There are cowboys all over the place and they'll put on a rodeo just for the hell of it."

But we didn't go to the saloon bar of the Willingdon Hotel in Okotoks to "talk to the boys." We approached the Millarville Racing and Agricultural Society. Set in the well-treed hills and dales southwest of Calgary and about twenty miles from Okotoks, Millarville is a widespread community of farms and ranches rather than a compact village. The Sheep River runs placidly through it in summer and fall, but rages through the valleys in the spring and early summer as the snow melts in the mountains, causing the spring run-off.

It is a beautiful place at any time of year, with mountain peaks tall behind the forests, and much of it seemed to be in our parish, so to speak. So when my fellow committeemember and I appeared by arrangement at the council meeting of the society, I was meeting old friends who wanted to know how Janet and I were reacting to city life and university work. But they did more than that.

They listened to our proposal and reacted favourably. On one point, however, they were adamant. They would organize not a rodeo with bucking broncos but a display of farming and ranching skills. It would be fun as well as interesting. They offered us the use of the Millarville Fairgrounds and Race-track. And, they suggested, the community hall could be used, too. Wouldn't we like to have a dance after the display? We would? That could be arranged! Not only that, but, we said with growing enthusiasm, the doctors had a very proficient orchestra. They could provide the music for such an occasion! And what about a barbecue, with that wonderful Alberta beef cooked in a specially prepared pit? Wouldn't we like that? We would? Done! we were told. It wasn't hard to change my earlier opinion of a barbecue.

But what about the display of farming and ranching skills, I asked. What would this consist of?

That was easily explained. They'd have team roping contests and other events. Roping is still a practical part of ranch work, especially when calves have to be braced. It calls for skill and expert timing, as riders flip their lassoes under calves' hooves and drag them quickly towards the branding fires. Nowadays teams compete with one another. So they'd have a competition which would interest spectators from faraway places, we were told.

We were leaving the hall, full of enthusiasm for the project, when somebody said to me, "Doc, you'll have to wear a western hat for this occasion. You've got to show them you're one of us, you know!"

In my enthusiasm to please, I was rash enough to say I would.

That summer, Janet and I had built a holiday cottage on the east coast of Vancouver Island. It would later become our retirement home. Built on a wooded cliff overlooking the sea, with bald eagles hovering far overhead and seals sunning themselves on the rocky beach, it is a beautiful and peaceful place, made all the more attractive by the welcome extended to us by our new neighbours.

But it is no longer the prairies. Wide-brimmed Stetsons are not often seen, and one evening over a glass of beer I made that observation to one of our new friends. He nodded in agreement, adding that as a prairie lad born and bred, he'd often regretted that he no longer owned a Stetson.

It was the very idea I'd been looking for. I'd been wanting in some way to acknowledge Erwin's many kindnesses, and how better than to present him with a western hat! Not only that, but I could kill two birds with one stone. I had no intention of spending good money to wear a hat on just one occasion, but if I wore it first and later presented it to my friend, two purposes would have been served in one fell swoop!

No sooner said than done. The hat I bought was not one of your touristy hats, known for what it is at first glance. The one I bought was the real McCoy. It cost real money. And it behoved me to take care of it.

So when the great day dawned and the buses drew into the Millarville Fairgrounds and Race-track bearing the guests of the Canadian Medical Association, I was there to greet them, resplendent in my Stetson. "And you've got to sit on a goddamn horse, too," someone had said.

I will always have fond memories of the Millarville race-track set amidst the low-lying foothills. On July first every year — Dominion Day or

Canada Day, whichever you please — it hosts the Millarville Races, an event that has now undoubtedly become more cosmopolitan than it was in the days when the track was surrounded by a sea of men wearing Stetsons. Now it is a popular holiday and picnic spot for city people pretending for the day to be cattlemen. Expensive horses now pound round the race-track.

But I remember a July first when a lady jockey — a rancher's wife — considered she'd been wronged (on the track, of course!), finished the race in third position instead of first, tethered her horse to the rail, walked across to where the winner stood and laid him flat with a right hook that would have drawn the admiration of Muhammad Ali himself.

And I remember how Janet, who had her little circle of admirers of the macho type she'd once so worried about, was approached by one of them who said surreptitiously, "Dr. Janet, put all you've got on Prairie Fire," adding, "to win."

Her winnings were substantial. But the Prairie Fire which won, it later transpired, was not Prairie Fire at all, but a faster substitute, with its markings slightly altered for that one occasion only. Later in the evening, apparently, the truth came out, and they say that the fist fight which ensued between one outraged owner and another is truly memorable. But that was all long ago, when honest rage seldom seemed to be accompanied by viciousness.

And some say Canada is dull!

Nor was our display of farming and ranching skills dull. But there was light entertainment too. The perverse antics of Stuart Sinclair-Smith's trained mule greatly amused the crowd. Our guests, seated on the steeply terraced seats that overlook the race-track, enjoyed it all, the quarter-horse races to the calf roping. Even if it was a colder day than we had anticipated, there was the community hall and the dance to follow.

I had planned to attend the dance, but first I felt I should thank the local people who had so generously worked to put on the events of the afternoon. Still wearing Erwin's Stetson, as I thought, I moved about, shaking hands with old friends, when I was invited into the infield to join the boys in a drink.

The infield at rodeos is where much of the real work takes place. Among the clutter of trucks and wagons, horses are unloaded or loaded, groomed or walked about, and harness is readied. When the day's events have ended, postmortems are held, and a certain spirit of conviviality takes over.

It is that spirit of conviviality that can make "having a drink in the infield'' a hazard of Western living. I had avoided it over the years and tried to decline this invitation by drawing attention to my duties to the medical society.

"Doc," said Jake Naseby, speaking confidentially, "you're expected. Besides," he added, not unkindly, and nodding towards the community hall, "there are going to be men in there tonight who're a helluva lot smarter than you to take care of things. Come on."

It was an invitation I simply couldn't refuse. Dusk was descending as we joined our friends in the infield. Horses were being walked about, gear being gathered and loaded on to trucks while a group of fellows were wiping down the steaming flanks of their mounts.

I had not eaten for hours. The evening had turned cold. I was glad of the offer of a drink from a hipflask. But you cannot drink with one fellow and not another. It's simply not done. So I had a little rye, a little rum, a taste of Scotch from a third fellow and — if I remember correctly — a little brandy, followed no doubt by a second tot of rum.

Suddenly I realized something was wrong. I felt light-headed, and immediately I knew the cause. I wasn't wearing my hat. It wasn't on my head.

"My hat!" I cried. "I've lost my hat!"

"No, you haven't," someone said. "You were wearing it ten minutes ago. It's between here and your car somewhere."

It was dark by now, but despite a sudden unaccountable feeling of weakness, the urge to find my — or Erwin's — hat was paramount.

Two of my companions offered to help me look. In looking for a hat in the dark, obviously one has to wend one's way rather than walk like a soldier on parade. Thus I was wending my way when suddenly my legs became strangely weak and I found myself face down on the ground, prostrate. I had quite literally bitten the dust.

Two strong men hoisted me to my feet.

"Your hat was in the car, Doc."

Near tragedy had been averted. My hat was saved.

I did not attend the dance that night, though I'm told it was a great success. I felt too delicate to go. I was exhausted by the labours of the day and glad to go home to bed murmuring the poet's words, "Tired Nature's sweet restorer, balmy sleep."

By morning I had recovered from my indisposition. Apprehension, however, held me in its grip. My only comfort was that Erwin would get his Stetson, not necessarily in a state of pristine purity, but still, he'd get it.

As to myself, the good name so carefully nurtured over the years had gone, dragged through the dirt. But I must show my face in public. Shame would not make me bow my head in the face of scorn or contempt. Besides, perhaps nobody knew about it.

We went to the Willumsens' for lunch that day as we usually did on Sundays. We were just about to seat ourselves at the dining room table when Norman, their elder son, a fellow of forty, asked me smilingly, "Are you feeling okay today, Doc?"

To which I immediately replied, "Just splendid, Norman, thank you."

"Well I'll tell you something, Doc," said Norman. "Your reputation's always been good around here, but that business of you falling flat on your face on the race-track last night has put you right on top, believe me!"

Chapter Forty-five

"The surgical removal of children's tonsils," declaimed the lecturer, a young specialist, to the class of forty or fifty students, "was never necessary. It was a ritualistic piece of surgery, exposing children to unwarranted risks."

He paused for effect.

"The only benefits of tonsillectomy were to line the pockets of doctors unscrupulous enough to carry out such operations."

I drew a deep breath and looked sideways at my companion, an ear, nose and throat surgeon.

When the University of Calgary opened its medical school in 1969, its program was almost revolutionary for such technological times. Family doctors were invited to teach medical students the art and practice of family medicine. It was a great honour for me, a middle-aged country general practitioner, to be appointed (no doubt because of my greying hair) an assistant professor.

Part-time, or clinical, faculty members receive little or no stipend. For a thousand years, doctors faithful to the oath of Hippocrates have believed it an honour and a duty to teach medical students. Calgary's "part-timers," general practitioners and specialists alike, were an enthusiastic lot.

Until that remark about the unwarranted financial rewards of the surgical removal of tonsils in children, I had been comfortable in my new role.

But now, listening to the dogmatic declaration of this young man, I wasn't too sure of myself.

After all, a mere ten years previously, as the operating room nurses were wheeling my third tonsillectomy case of the morning into the operating theatre, one of them had said to me cheerfully, "Dr. Gibson, you must be the Tonsillectomy King of the Foothills!"

For I had removed many tonsils and adenoids in High River. There wasn't time or room enough in Calgary hospitals to carry out this operation, and so cases were referred by city doctors to doctors working in smaller hospitals in the surrounding countryside. I received my fair share of such referrals, hence the nurse's cheery quip.

Yet I was proud of my record. I believed that I had never operated needlessly and I never had real trouble with any patient, though sometimes I had anxious moments, for tonsillectomy is wrongly considered minor surgery. Perhaps the anaesthetist takes even more responsibility than the surgeon, as throat surgery is delicate work and a clear breathing channel is vital. That is the anaesthetist's, as much as the surgeon's, responsibility.

So I sat there, listening and fuming. An occasional glance at the throat surgeon's impassive face afforded me no comfort.

We recruits to teaching had been advised to attend lectures when we could, and I found great interest in having old ideas challenged. But this one was a bit more than I cared to take. At the end of the lecture, as the students swarmed out of the class, I turned to my companion, the throat surgeon, "Well I'll be damned," I said, "but I felt insulted by that chap's remarks. You don't believe that stuff, do you?"

My friend, who had known me for many years, merely smiled.

"Don't worry," he said. "It's one man's opinion. I'll give mine tomorrow. Besides," he added with a grin, "you'd be surprised at how many young specialists want me to take their kids' tonsils out."

So, half placated, I went my way, but thoughtfully. It was one man's opinion all right, but it was the opinion of inexperience. The lecturer, for all his qualifications, was too young to have seen the abominably filthy, dangerously infected tonsils of fifteen or twenty years before, when chronically enlarged and infected tonsils could lead to all kinds of illnesses, from simple but dangerous obstruction to the breathing passage, to acute ear infections or even the once dreaded rheumatic fever.

In our student days in Glasgow, slum children suffered terribly from tonsillar infections. They ate poorly, slept badly, snored in their sleep like old men, and developed chains of infected glands in their necks. And that was the least of it.

Surgical removal of their tonsils often worked wonders for their health, and as I drove the thirty miles from the university to Okotoks, I pondered the whole question of the changing face of medicine.

One thing that had puzzled and surprised Janet and me in our first months in Okotoks was the number and severity of chronically infected tonsils we saw. In the slums of Glasgow or industrial England, yes, that was understandable. But in the fresh, clean air of the Canadian prairies?

And then, perhaps, the answer and the cure. Many country people in the 1950s were still living in the small settlers' homes their parents had built, overheated in winter by old furnaces. The air became extremely dry and hot, continually irritating little ones' throats. But by the middle of the 1960s, with increasing affluence and modern homes with adequate humidity in the air, I and my colleagues saw fewer and fewer purulent tonsils. Early treatment of tonsillitis with antibiotics was, of course, another great help.

So I forgave the young man his opinion, and arrived at High River hospital a week or so later to remove the tonsils of a five-year-old. It was fast becoming an uncommon operation, but with years of experience behind me, I felt no qualms about operating.

It was one of those dark winter mornings for which the prairies are notorious. The snow was driving along almost horizontally before the wind, and the windshield wipers of my jeep were working overtime, but I had allowed for the snow and arrived at the hospital in good time, changed into operating room greens and opened the door to the O.R. just as the anaesthetist, my old friend Dr. Cliff Forsyth, said, "You can start in a few minutes."

Our little patient lay breathing quietly, safely, and the operation commenced. I removed one tonsil and inspected the tonsil bed for any bleeding that might have occurred.

"It's blowing up into a blizzard," said Cliff, as the hard snow lashed against the operating room window.

And then the lights went out. The storm had caused a power cut. For a few moments until the auxiliary lighting came on, we would be in the dark.

There was immediate controlled panic. Peggy Murphy, our operating room director, friend and colleague of many years, called for storm lamps. Her nurses responded immediately to her orders.

It was a dangerous moment, for bleeding, unseen, undetected, could become uncontrolled and catastrophic. Forsyth and I bent to our duties. It was a situation that called for calmness, for decision, for leadership — even for command — and as the surgeon, I rose to the challenge.

"Don't worry," I exclaimed. "If necessary, like Walter Mitty, I shall operate in the dark."

"That's right, ladies," said Dr. Forsyth in tones of great confidence, "you needn't worry about Gibson. He's in his element. He's been operating in the dark for ten years!"

Chapter Forty-six

In September 1969, almost thirty years to the day that Janet and I had qualified as doctors, Catriona was killed in a car accident.

She was twenty-six. She was a barrister who, we were told by her dean of law, had faced a brilliant future. She had graduated with distinction three years before, the first woman student at Queen's University Law School to gain the top marks in her class for each year of the course.

She was the first woman lawyer to be appointed as legal counsel to a major international oil company in western Canada, but was offered a scholarship to return to academic studies at Osgoode Hall Law School in Toronto to take the postgraduate degree of master of laws, specializing in industrial relations. She accepted the offer and the challenge. She had attended a convention in northern Ontario and was driving back to classes when the accident occurred. She was alone in her car and died instantly.

Catriona was a quiet and sensitive little girl and a perceptive, loyal and attractive young woman. When the three of us left Britain in 1955 to begin a new life in Canada, she talked of us as "the team" and when, a year later, our new Canadian friend Mrs. Rowan died and her eleven-year-old daughter Mary came to live with us, Mary "joined the team."

Her loyalty to those she loved was absolute. Even when she was a child she had made us proud of her achievements, but far more than that, she had given us love and brought meaning and joy to our lives. She was the centre of our existence. For twenty-six years Janet and I had shared a beautiful dream, and now it was over.

Perhaps Wordsworth spoke for so many like Janet and myself when he wrote:

Thanks to the human heart by which we live,
Thanks to its tenderness, its joys, and fears,
To me the meanest flower that blows can give
Thoughts that do often lie too deep for tears.

We had seen tragedy only too often in our lives. For years, said Janet, we had had to tell people in circumstances like our own that there is no panacea for grief. Now we must show our community that we could face our own sorrow.

We continued with our work, but we were seldom left alone. Friends and neighbours surrounded us. Catriona's young friends invaded our house, mingling with the older people. Three young men travelled across Canada to be with us.

It was the young people, especially, who made us realize that we must not let them down by showing weakness. By doing so we would only betray Catriona who, they told us, had so often spoken to them of our strength.

But such kindness gave us strength. I have not forgotten the farmer who walked up to our door, thrust a bottle of whisky at me, gripped my arm and, wordless, walked away. Nor will we forget the steady stream of casual visitors who phoned to say they were bringing food and who would sit unobtrusively for a while, or do some little chore that might help Janet, and as quietly as they had come, go away.

It was years later that we learned that our "casual" visitors had been organized so that we would not be alone too much.

Mary and Catriona had been inseparable and Mary, married by now, showed us how much she cared. She seldom left our side. One day she saddled the horses, brought them to the door and pleaded with me to come riding. Janet, her friends beside her, urged me to go with Mary, and we rode for hours together across the foothills Catriona had loved so much. Mary rode quietly beside me, letting me talk if I wanted to, and in the end, though I had dreaded going, I found some peace.

Catriona's young friends are scattered and older now, but they remain our friends and can still smile as they remember the happy days of years ago.

We may love our children deeply. They may be the light of our lives, but we may not truly know them, their thoughts and aspirations until they begin to mature; at least so it was with myself and Catriona. She had been very bright at school, was the top student of her graduating year at the Okotoks High School and went on to take an arts degree, but surprised me when she quietly told us that she wanted to study law. By that time I recognized how competitive and how determined to excel this attractive little person was.

And she excelled in more than academic matters.

One day a rancher watching Catriona and Mary, teenagers then, put the horses through their paces, said, "You know, Doc, these two girls of yours are among the best horsewomen in this countryside!"

And how can I forget the evening they arrived home, exultant, their blue jeans almost rigid with mud, their hair full of straw, and I, aghast, cried, "Where on earth have you two been?" to receive the answer "Out" as they shot into their bedroom and hastily closed the door.

It was Janet who appeased me.

"They've been up at Ruth Fuller's place." She smiled serenely.

"You needn't worry," she said. "The boys are practising for the junior steer riding competitions and you don't think that pair are going to let boys off with anything, do you?"

The girls had been steer riding with the best of them!

But the teenage stage passed and I began to see Catriona's full potential. No challenge was too much for her. She was an excellent mathematician and had, so I was told, a brilliant analytical mind. Perhaps that is what drew her to the study of law.

It is over now, but for millions like us it will never be over as long as we live. We never wholly lose those we have loved. Perhaps Janet put it best when she said one day, "Catriona lives in the jewel box of my memory."

And so it will always be for both of us.

Chapter Forty-seven

"What's this I hear about you leaving Okotoks, Doc? Is it true?" asked my patient before he'd even sat down. He was in town on business, but heard the rumour and decided to investigate, hence the visit to my office.

We had known one another for years and were old friends. I nodded and waved him to a chair.

"It's true, Al. Janet and I are moving into Calgary. It's time for a change. We've had a wonderful life here but things haven't been the same for us for this last year or so. You know that."

Despite all the kindness and warmth that was showered upon us, country practice can be a wearing and sometimes a lonely business. One night a few months after Catriona's death, I was called to the hospital at High River. The thirty-mile round trip, on a lonely, snowbound road was no pleasure. In the blinding snow a heavy truck nearly struck my car. I got home in the very early hours of the morning, and Janet was sitting waiting for me by a fire that had long gone out. There and then I knew we should move.

But we made up our minds to find a doctor for the town before we went. At last Okotoks was beginning to grow. There were about a thousand people living there and the town's future growth seemed assured.

But the Skye Glen schoolhouse as a clinic was too small. We would have to do something about that. My friend Dr. Donald McNeil, one of Calgary's senior specialists in medicine, recommended to us a young physician who might be interested in coming to Okotoks. He saw the possibilities, accepted our offer, and together we bought My Wigwam, a restaurant on Okotoks's business street. We hired an architect and soon we had created an attractive clinic, the waiting room capacious, quietly carpeted and restful, with potted plants arranged around the walls, and furnished with antiques and paintings carefully selected by Janet.

But for us it was a temporary thing, and our friends and our young colleague knew that. As soon as he was established in practice, we would move to the city.

And so, as my friend Al sat there asking about our leaving, it was easy to tell him that I had been offered work as a sessional physician at the university's Students' Health Service in Calgary.

"Is that so?" said my visitor. "Well, the day I'm sick I'll have to be a student at the university, won't I?"

Since he was in his late fifties, a grizzled and weatherbeaten cattleman ranching in the foothills a good thirty miles southwest of Calgary, I assured him that he would find it far more suitable to come to our partner, a capable physician, than try to find me in Calgary. He would think about it, he said, and made to take his leave.

"Al," I called after him, "they won't let you see me. I'll be a university employee. They'll only let registered students be seen at the health service!"

"Well," growled Al, "we'll see about that. Maybe the day I'm sick I'll have to be a registered student."

And he was gone.

Janet and I moved into a pleasant suite of rooms in the city. Mary and her husband also lived in Calgary. Janet, after more than thirty years of active practice, decided to take at least a prolonged vacation, and I began my new job.

I was fortunate in having Dr. Donald McNeil as director of the health service. I was one of several doctors who worked there under his guidance, and since he was a senior specialist in medicine it was a tremendous change for me to be able to get an expert's advice by simply walking from one room to another! The university's well-equipped sick bay, with its staff of professional nurses, was a short walk from the clinic and my duties there were interesting and challenging, with new patients and new problems.

Catriona had once told me that I was the kind of person who should be working in a students' health service. "Kids seem able to talk to you, Dad," she had said, and in a strange way I found comfort in being able to work with young people.

One day, a year or so later, when I was examining a very pretty young student who had just begun her university studies, I said to her, "You know, I almost feel I've met you before."

She smiled at me. "Well, I wasn't going to say anything, Doctor," she said, "but you certainly have. You delivered me. And then years later you took out my appendix! But we moved away from Okotoks. So you see, I'm really just an old patient of yours!"

*

A good deal of my work at the health service seemed to involve dealing with medical problems caused by stress.

Young people were often away from home for the first time; family values were often replaced by those of the peer group, and these were not always in the best interests of naive youngsters who at the same time sometimes found the educational standards of the universities to be far more exacting than they had expected. Then, of course, there were the inevitable emotional problems, as well as ordinary illnesses.

For many years I had believed that stress, both mental and physical, was a necessary and also a beneficial part of living. While too much physical stress can certainly be harmful, its effects are mild as compared to the ravages of frustration, anger, resentment, grief, unresolved worry or ambition. In some way, unrelieved stress, I conjectured, could upset the fine balance of the body's ability to cope with disease and infection. Even young students were not immune to this process, I believed.

One day when giving a lecture, I philosophized along these lines to my audience of medical students. It was conjecture, of course, but based on years of observation. Why, for instance, do so many middle-aged, apparently healthy men who lose their wives, die for no obvious reason a year or so later? Why does illness often accompany or follow bitter family quarrels?

A colleague who was present challenged my remarks.

"You have no statistical proof that such a statement about stress is true," he declared, and I was forced to agree that such was the case, for although Dr. Hans Selye's work on the subject was then internationally known, he still had his critics.

However, as I reminded my colleague, Pasteur had precious little proof that bacteria caused disease when he began the work that would make medicine as much a science as an art.

And I also reminded him of the doctor who broke the handle off the public well in one of London's boroughs a century or so ago. He had no statistical proof that the scores of people dying from what must have been cholera were drinking infected water from that well, but he stopped the epidemic, even if he landed in jail for his trouble.

Becoming a little peeved as I warmed to my response, I next quoted Sir Winston Churchill's remark, made in another context, that there are three kinds of lies — lies, damned lies, and statistics! In a profession such as medicine there is a need for conjectural philosophizing at times, for so many of our problems are unsolved mysteries, even to the most learned of clinicians and research workers.

None is more of a mystery than the human brain — and as for the human mind, whatever that is, and how it controls our well-being...! On the other hand, for many years it had been unchallenged dogma that most mental diseases are caused by psychological trauma, by deep mental hurt. These beliefs have been put forward as fact, and physicians who suggested that there might be physical or biochemical causes for some mental illnesses have been dismissed as heretics. Powerful forces and distinguished men arraigned themselves against such dissidents, and their voices were stifled.

Schizophrenia is a case in point. For decades this illness was considered to lie within the unchallenged domain of psychological analysts. Only recently has science entered the scene. Brains of sufferers from this and other diseases have been stored for many years in pathology departments. They are being studied by teams of neurologists, psychiatrists, neuroanatomists, computer experts and other scientists.

This work is being undertaken at a number of research centres including the University of Calgary Medical School. By using modern sophisticated techniques, research workers are beginning to gather evidence that sufferers from schizophrenia have had an illness like any other, but one caused by micro-organisms attacking the brain.

True, they don't as yet have statistical proof, but they can conjecture with some reason — and surely that is necessary in the study of mental upset, whose causes are complex and varied. There is no room for dogma. Medicine is constantly changing. The challenge is always there as bacteria, and now the viruses, show their versatility and deadly ability to change their ways as they prey on their human hosts.

But I wasn't involved in any philosophical discussion on stress when one morning I heard voices raised in the corridor outside my office. I was dealing with nothing more exotic than a bruised thumb.

Months had passed since I first began to work at the university. It was winter and snowing hard. I recognized both voices. One belonged to my nurse and the other to an old friend.

"Just a minute, then," nurse was saying, "and I'll speak to him."

There was a knock at the door. Nurse came in. She's a pretty woman and a very easy person to work with, but she was a bit flustered and her face was flushed.

"Dr. Gibson," she began agitatedly, "there's an enormous cowboy out there who says he's —"

"I know," I interrupted her. "He says he's a registered student at this university and he has to see me."

When he came in, still wearing his Stetson and the padded jacket that most ranchers wear in cold weather, Al remarked that I was well protected against intruders.

"Did I ever have a job getting past that nurse!" he said. "I could just walk into your office in Okotoks, but it's sure as hell different here!"

"Al," I reminded him, "I told you it wouldn't be easy to see me in this place, and besides, the nurse is doing what she's supposed to do. And you've got to admit, you don't look much like a student."

Since he was on the wrong side of fifty, stood about six feet three, had a bit of weight on and was wearing the kind of clothes that marked him as a rancher to all but the blind, one could sympathize with the nurse's dilemma.

"Amazing," I said. "Don't tell me you've driven here just to say hello. What's going on?"

"It's this pain my chest, Doc," replied my friend. "I don't like it. It's maybe just wind, but if it is I can't bring it up. And I don't feel all that good either. So I thought I'd come and see you. Tell the nurse I'm sorry, but I sure as hell wasn't going to go away 'til I'd seen you."

Like most of his kind, he would not bother to seek help for anything minor. The obvious thing was a heart attack of some kind and I began to question him.

"Do you have pain in your arm, Al — your left arm especially — or your right?"

"No."

"Pain in your wrist or your elbow, or your neck, or your jaw?"

"No."

"Have you been breathless?"

"No."

My enquiries were not helpful, and when eventually I asked him to strip and examined him, there was nothing much there either. His heart sounds were normal and so was his blood pressure.

Still, I knew my friend of old. By anyone's standards he was physically a very tough character, and if anything he'd deny pain rather than admit it. His ideas on pain would be associated with the likes of a broken leg, not a trifle like "a bit of wind in the chest." And yet he'd been worried enough to drive a long way in bad weather.

Something was going on, my clinical instinct told me, and I telephoned one of the heart specialists who listened to my suspicions, then said we should admit my patient to hospital for observation. He'd do an electrocardiograph on admission, he told me, and he'd let me know.

"Negative," he said when he phoned me several hours later. "Still, we'll keep him in until we get another ECG tomorrow."

But it was a different story the next day. A second electrocardiograph and the accompanying tests proved that Al had had a coronary infarct and he was kept in hospital for several weeks, where I visited him from time to time.

In those weeks my own fortunes took an unexpected turn. It was suggested to me that if I applied for the new position of professor and head of the Division of Family Practice, my application would be given favourable consideration.

I was astounded, flattered and at the same time perturbed. I was very happy working as a doctor at the health service. I would have to give that up, and I would also have to forgo the university summer vacation that lasted from May until September. Unlike the rest of the university, the medical school did not close during the summer months. And I did not need to be told that the work would be both hard and time-consuming.

I was no academic. I was a practising family doctor, hardly the type to inhabit the groves of academe. I wasn't much of a conformist either, but I did have strong views about family doctoring, and so I demurred. But my sessions at the health service would not be terminated; they would be reduced, I was told, and I would receive adequate holiday time.

Since holiday time for us had usually meant ten days annually and those often delayed because someone wouldn't have her baby according to schedule, the dean's proposal seemed like a G.P.'s view of paradise.

Janet and I held a conference, including Mary and our close friends, the consensus being that I should take the job if it was offered to me and get on with it.

After many interviews with members of the faculty — and not all of them favourable by any means — I was appointed to this new post.

I visited Al in hospital. Three weeks had passed since I had him admitted on a hunch more than anything else. He was recovering nicely and after talking with the cardiologist, it was agreed that he could go home the next day.

"Do I get to come and see you, Doc?" he asked me. "And if I do, will they try to stop me?"

"No, Al. You see, everything's changed these last few weeks. You'll be able to come and see me at the Health Sciences Centre at the university. I'll have an office there. Only — you'll have to agree to having medical students or young doctors examine you."

"How's that, Doc?"

"Well, you see, Al, I'll be teaching there — teaching students and young M.D.s about family medicine. And having them examine patients under my supervision is one of the conditions of the job."

"What job?"

"Well, Al, they've made me a professor, d'ye see."

I could see Al was mentally digesting this piece of news as I took my leave of him after telling him to come for a check-up in two weeks' time.

He duly appeared two weeks later, saying he felt just fine, and I got down to the business not only of examining him but of instructing him as to his future life style, advice which I knew very well he'd take under advisement, accepting or rejecting my recommendations cheerfully and with good will.

My two students listened as I expounded on the symptoms, signs and perhaps the causes of impending heart trouble. Then they examined my friend. He took all this in good part, until finally I thanked the two young people for their attention and said they might go.

"Here! Just a minute," exclaimed the patient. "I'm part of this, you know! I've got a right to be heard and I've got something to say to you two people," nodding at the students. "Kin I say somethin', Doc?" he asked me.

"Sure, Al," I agreed, taken aback, yet realizing that he was perfectly within his rights in speaking up, and that perhaps unconsciously I had correctly been rebuked.

"Well, then," continued the rancher, "I'll tell you what doctorin's all about. Trust. That's what it's all about. If you don't trust your doctor, you got nothin'. Some doctors never learn that patients need t' trust them. Now I'm one man that doesn't trust every guy in the world. Ah'll tell y' that, too. But," he said, pointing at me, "I trust this guy here. I came thirty miles in a snowstorm so's I could see him. Because I trusted him, see?"

It was manna from heaven. Here I was, appointed as head of a department whose very existence was based on the need to tempt young doctors to go into family practice. And here was a chap doing my job for me! What a delight. The students were impressed, and, as for me, I was getting swelled headed!

Finally the consultation was over. The students took their leave and Al began to clip up his shirt front. For some reason cowboy shirts have clips, not buttons, and Al was clipping his shirt up slowly and audibly, looking at me all the while, I thought, in a most peculiar manner.

"Al," I said finally, disturbed by his searching gaze, "something's got you worrying. What is it?"

"Hell no, Doc, I'm not worryin'. But I will admit I'm wonderin'."

"Wondering? What about?"

"I'm wonderin', Doc," he said, "how in hell do they make a professor out of a little guy like you?"

Epilogue

It is probably true to say that doctors of my generation have seen the practice of medicine become more a science than an art.

Until about 1937 when the first sulphonamides were used clinically to combat acute infections, doctors were virtually helpless in dealing with them. The sulphonamides, forerunners of the antibiotics that appeared about eight years later, could literally kill bacteria, and as the first drugs to do so, they were discovered by scientists, not by physicians.

In 1937, as a medical student, I remember seeing a child, desperately ill and dying from meningitis. At that time the death rate in children from this dreaded disease approached 90 per cent. I have never forgotten how the professor of medicine, who had been given a small quantity of this drug on a trial basis, gave it to this little girl. It was her last hope and a gamble on his part — a gamble in which he had nothing to lose.

The cure was dramatic. Turning to the small group of students around him, Professor Glen said quietly that we had witnessed not a miracle but the use of a new drug. With its use, he said, the future of medicine had passed into the hands of the scientists, rather than the physicians.

His words were prophetic. Science has indeed given us wonderful weapons with which to fight disease. Old Dr. Duff, years before that, had sensed the future when he told me that as a doctor I would live to see wonders of medicine and surgery performed one day.

I still possess a small handbook written for general practitioners and published fifty years ago. It is called *The Art and Practice of Medicine* and is only a collectible now. I smile sometimes when I look at the prescriptions recommended in it for various conditions and diseases. Although those ingredients have long since been discredited scientifically as having any therapeutic value whatsoever, they *did* have value. That value lay in the human sympathy, support and reassurance given by the physician who prescribed them, and that should never be underestimated in these scientific times.

I used to say that much of the value of the family doctor lay in his good diagnostic and clinical sense — and supportive reassurance. I'm not so sure that the remark still isn't true, even with all the tremendous advantages that science has bestowed upon us.

We have a new understanding of the scientific basis of medicine, and because of this, millions are alive today who would otherwise have died. And science must go on with its painstaking, exacting and impersonal research, for without it, millions in the future may die of diseases as yet dormant or undiscovered.

But science by its very nature is impersonal. The object of science is to discover the truth. "Statistical proof" is immensely important in the work of scientists and is essential to their research, if in the end it is to benefit mankind.

The trouble sometimes is that doctors, in universities and out of them, have become overawed by science, and pay great homage to it, neglecting the art of medicine in its favour. We sometimes forget that the practice of medicine is by its nature a very human and personal affair.

When people are ill they are often, in a sense, disadvantaged. In a way they feel at our mercy, sometimes humiliated by their illnesses, angry and afraid. And sometimes they are in despair. In hospitals, surrounded by all the strange, scientific life-saving apparatus that is available today. In such circumstances, patients often feel isolated at a most grievous time in their lives, away from family and friends.

Science may save their lives, but the old art of medical practice has its place in speeding the healing process. The power of the human mind is immeasurable, and so, therefore, is the part it plays in healing disease. If this is sometimes scientifically underestimated, it is there all the same, and we doctors must always remind ourselves of this.

The art of medicine must go hand in hand with the science, for if we rely on science too much, we can end in trouble. For instance, we sometimes use medications too trustingly and too casually. For all their benefits they can be dangerous. Just as there is no such person as a doctor who has never made a mistake, there is no such thing as a completely safe drug.

Penicillin, the wonder drug that has saved millions of lives, has also killed thousands. Even the lowly painkillers can harm as well as help.

Iatrogenic medicine — the study of illness or symptoms brought about by medication or medical care — is a new and thriving branch of my profession.

Perhaps we could do worse than recall the words of Napoleon when he said to his doctor, "We are machines made to live — organized expressly for that purpose. Such is our nature. Do not counteract the living principle. Leave it at liberty to defend itself and it will do better than your drugs: Doctor — no Medicine."

Napoleon had a point.

And so had Sir William Osler, the great Canadian doctor, when he said, "One of the first duties of the physician to to educate the masses not to take medicine."